Preface.. 13

What You Will Learn..15

How to Use This Book for Maximum Benefit...16

Chapter 1.. 18

Basic Formulas and Functions..............................18

Understanding Formulas:...........................18

Creating a Simple Formula:...................... 18

Using Functions:..................................... 19

Common Functions:................................. 20

Copying Formulas and Functions:........... 20

Understanding Cell References:.............. 21

Saving and Organising Excel Files................. 21

Saving Your Workbook for the First Time:..22

AutoSave Feature:................................... 22

Organising Your Excel Files:..................... 23

Opening and Closing Workbooks:............23

Backing Up Your Work:............................ 24

Chapter 2.. 25

Basic Formulas and Functions..........................25

Introduction to Formulas: Sum, Average, Min, Max... 25

Summing Numbers:................................. 25

Finding Averages:.................................... 26

Identifying Minimum and Maximum Values:.. 26

Understanding Cell References: Relative, Absolute, and Mixed................................26

Relative Cell References:....................27

Absolute Cell References:...................27

Mixed Cell References:.......................28

Basic Functions: COUNT, SUMIF, AVERAGEIF...28

COUNT:...28

SUMIF:..28

AVERAGEIF:.......................................29

Understanding Cell References: Relative, Absolute, and Mixed.....................................29

Relative Cell References:...........................30

Absolute Cell References:.........................30

Mixed Cell References:.............................31

How to Use Them:....................................31

Basic Functions: COUNT, SUMIF, AVERAGEIF. 32

COUNT:...33

SUMIF:..33

AVERAGEIF:.......................................34

Chapter 3... 36

Logical Functions.. 36

Using IF, AND, OR Functions for Decision-Making...36

IF Function:...36

AND Function:...37

OR Function:...37

Nested IFs and Using IF with Other Functions... 38

Nested IFs:...38

Using IF with Other Functions:.......................38

Nested IFs and Using IF with Other Functions... 39

Nested IFs for Multiple Conditions:........... 40

Combining IF with AND/OR:..................... 40

Using IF with Other Functions:................. 41

Tips for Working with Nested IFs and Complex Formulas:..................................... 42

Chapter 4... **43**

Lookup Functions................................... **43**

VLOOKUP and HLOOKUP Basics................. 43

VLOOKUP Basics:................................... 43

HLOOKUP Basics:.................................. 44

Introduction to INDEX and MATCH for Flexible Lookups... 45

INDEX Function:...................................... 45

MATCH Function:.................................... 46

Combining INDEX and MATCH:..................... 46

Chapter 5... **48**

Date and Time Functions........................ **48**

Working with Dates and Times: TODAY, NOW, DATE, DATEDIF.. 48

TODAY Function:..................................... 48

NOW Function:.. 49

DATE Function:....................................... 49

DATEDIF Function:.................................. 50

Calculating Differences Between Dates, Working with Workdays................................... 50

NETWORKDAYS Function:...................... 51

Calculating Differences Between Dates, Working with Workdays................................... 52

NETWORKDAYS Function:...................... 52

NETWORKDAYS.INTL Function:............53

WORKDAY Function:...........................54

WORKDAY.INTL Function:....................54

Chapter 6..**56**

Data Organisation...............................**56**

Sorting and Filtering Data.............................56

Sorting Data:...56

Filtering Data:..57

Data Validation for Input Control....................57

Setting Up Data Validation:.......................58

Creating Drop-Down Lists:........................58

Input Messages and Error Alerts:.............59

Practical Applications:..................................59

Chapter 7..**61**

PivotTables..**61**

Creating PivotTables for Data Summary.........61

What is a PivotTable?...............................61

Steps to Create a PivotTable:....................62

Customising PivotTables: Grouping, Calculated Fields...62

Grouping Data:...63

Adding Calculated Fields:........................ 63

Slicers and Timelines for Interactive Filtering. 63

Slicers:..63

Timelines:...64

Customising PivotTables: Grouping, Calculated Fields...65

Grouping Data in PivotTables:...................65

Adding Calculated Fields to PivotTables:.. 66

Slicers and Timelines for Interactive Filtering. 66

Using Slicers for Easy Filtering:................ 67

Implementing Timelines for Date Filtering:67

Slicers and Timelines for Interactive Filtering. 68

Slicers for Categorical Data Filtering.........69

How to Add Slicers:............................69

Customising Slicers:............................69

Connecting Slicers to Multiple PivotTables:...70

Timelines for Time-Based Data Filtering... 70

How to Add Timelines:.........................70

Customising Timelines:........................71

Benefits of Using Slicers and Timelines:. 71

Chapter 8... 73

Advanced Functions and Formulas.................. 73

Array Formulas for Complex Calculations.......73

Array Formulas:...................................73

Using SUMPRODUCT for Multi-Condition Sums 74

SUMPRODUCT Function:.........................74

Syntax and Use:...................................75

Example of SUMPRODUCT:...............75

Dynamic Named Ranges for Flexible Formulas.. 75

Dynamic Named Ranges:.........................75

Creating a Dynamic Named Range:....76

Example of Creating a Dynamic Named Range:...76

Using SUMPRODUCT for Multi-Condition Sums 77

Syntax and Use:...................................77

Dynamic Named Ranges for Flexible Formulas.. 78

Creating a Dynamic Named Range:......... 78

Dynamic Named Ranges for Flexible Formulas.. 80

Implementing Dynamic Named Ranges....80

Using OFFSET with COUNTA/COUNT:... 80

Expanding Beyond Single Columns:...81

Benefits and Uses of Dynamic Named Ranges.....................................81

Best Practices for Dynamic Named Ranges. 82

Chapter 9.. 84

Introduction to Macros and VBA...................... 84

Recording Basic Macros for Repetitive Tasks.84

How to Record a Macro:.......................... 84

Running Your Macro:...............................85

Tips for Effective Macro Recording:.......... 86

Brief Introduction to VBA for Automation.. 86

What is VBA?..................................... 86

Accessing the VBA Editor:................. 87

Writing a Simple VBA Macro:............. 87

Learning VBA:.. 88

Brief Introduction to VBA for Automation........ 88

Understanding VBA...............................89

What is VBA?..................................... 89

Why Use VBA?..................................89

Getting Started with VBA........................ 90

Accessing the VBA Editor:................. 90

Writing Your First Macro:.....................90

Understanding VBA Syntax:...............91

Automating Tasks with VBA.....................91

Looping and Conditionals:....................91

Interacting with Excel Objects:............91

Error Handling:....................................92

Advancing Your VBA Skills.....................92

Resources for Learning VBA:..............92

Chapter 10.. **94**

Charts and Graphs.................................**94**

Creating and Customising Charts: Bar, Line, Pie, and More...94

Creating Charts in Excel:..........................94

Customising Charts:............................95

Advanced Chart Techniques: Combo Charts, Secondary Axis...96

Combo Charts:..96

Using a Secondary Axis:.....................96

Chart Design Tips:...............................97

Advanced Chart Techniques: Combo Charts, Secondary Axis...98

Combo Charts..98

What Are Combo Charts?...................98

Creating a Combo Chart:....................99

Using a Secondary Axis...........................100

When to Use a Secondary Axis:........100

Adding a Secondary Axis:.................100

Tips for Effective Combo Charts and Secondary Axes.......................................101

Chapter 11...**103**

Conditional Formatting............................. **103**

Highlighting Data Dynamically..................... 103

What Is Dynamic Highlighting?......... 103

Applying Conditional Formatting:...... 104

Advanced Formatting Options...............105

Data Bars:... 105

Colour Scales:............................105

Icon Sets:.. 106

Tips for Using Conditional Formatting..... 106

Data Bars, Color Scales, and Icon Sets........107

Data Bars.. 107

What Are Data Bars?....................... 107

Applying Data Bars:...........................108

Colour Scales...108

What Are Color Scales?................... 108

Using Color Scales:...........................109

Icon Sets.. 109

What Are Icon Sets?....................... 109

Implementing Icon Sets:...................109

Tips for Advanced Conditional Formatting.... 110

Chapter 12..**112**

Conditional Formatting.............................**112**

Highlighting Data Dynamically......................112

Dynamic Highlighting with Conditional Formatting:....................................... 112

Steps to Apply Conditional Formatting:... 113

Advanced Visualisation with Data Bars, Color Scales, and Icon Sets................... 114

Data Bars:................................114

Colour Scales:............................. 114

Icon Sets:................................115

Tips for Using Conditional Formatting
Effectively.............................. 115

Managing and Editing Conditional Formatting
Rules.............................. 116

Reviewing Existing Conditional Formatting
Rules..................... 117

Steps to Review Conditional Formatting
Rules:.............................. 117

Editing Conditional Formatting Rules...... 117

How to Edit a Rule:............................118

Deleting Conditional Formatting Rules....118

Steps to Delete a Rule:......................119

Tips for Effective Conditional Formatting
Rule Management.............................. 119

Chapter 13.......................... **121**

Dashboards and Reporting...........................**121**

Principles of Effective Dashboards.............. 121

Clarity and Purpose:..........................121

Audience-Centric Design:..................122

Data Visualisation Choices:..............122

Interactivity and Flexibility:................. 123

Accuracy and Timeliness:................. 123

Performance Optimisation:...............123

Implementing Dashboard Principles in Excel
124

Integrating charts, PivotTables, and Conditional
Formatting.................................125

Integrating Charts..............................125

Choosing the Right Chart Types:....... 125

Dynamic Chart Data:........................ 126

Leveraging PivotTables.......................... 126

Summarising Data:........................... 126

Integrating with Charts – PivotCharts:..... 126

Slicers for Interactivity:...................... 126

Applying Conditional Formatting............. 127

Highlighting Key Data:....................... 127

Interactive Data Exploration:............. 127

Best Practices for Integration................. 127

Maintain a Clean Layout:................... 128

Ensure Consistency:......................... 128

Optimise for Performance:................ 128

Interactive controls (Form Controls, ActiveX)129

Form Controls................................... 129

Introduction to Form Controls:........... 129

Using Form Controls in Dashboards: 130

Implementing Form Controls:............ 130

ActiveX Controls..................................... 131

Introduction to ActiveX Controls:........ 131

Incorporating ActiveX Controls:......... 131

Implementing ActiveX Controls:........ 132

Best Practices for Using Interactive Controls
132

Chapter 14.. 134

Efficiency Boosters............................. 134

Keyboard Shortcuts for Navigation............... 134

Move Between Cells:......................... 134

Sheet Navigation:............................. 135

Navigating Within a Cell:................... 135

Keyboard Shortcuts for Formatting......... 135

Apply Basic Formats:....................... 135

Adjust Cell Formats:.......................... 136

Adjust Column Width and Row Height:... 136

Keyboard Shortcuts for Formulas........... 136

Entering and Editing Formulas:......... 136

Function Insertion:............................ 137

Formula Auditing:............................. 137

General Productivity Boosters................ 137

Quick Access to Ribbon Commands: 137

Creating a New Worksheet:.............. 137

Saving Your Workbook:..................... 137

Tips for Faster Data Entry............................ 138

Utilise Excel Tables:.......................... 138

AutoFill for Repetitive Data:.............. 139

Flash Fill for Pattern Recognition:..... 139

Data Validation for Consistency:........ 139

Tips for Efficient Data Editing.................. 140

Find and Replace for Quick Edits:..... 140

Use Formulas for Mass Updates:...... 140

Keyboard Shortcuts for Editing:......... 140

Leverage Sorting and Filtering:......... 140

General Efficiency Practices................... 141

Keep a Clean Workspace:................. 141

Use Templates for Recurring Projects:.... 141

Batch Process with Macros:.............. 141

Chapter 15.. 143

Troubleshooting Common Problems..............143

Dealing with Common Errors in Formulas.... 143

#DIV/0! Error - Division by Zero:....... 143

#NAME? Error - Unrecognized Text in Formulas:.. 144

#VALUE! Error - Incorrect Argument Type or Operand:............................ 144

#REF! Error - Invalid Cell Reference: 145

#N/A Error - No Value Available:........ 145

Circular Reference Warning:............. 145

Additional Tips for Troubleshooting Formulas.. 146

Using Formula Auditing Tools:...........146

Watching Cell Values:.......................146

Preface

Welcome to a journey through the world of Microsoft Excel, a tool that, despite its widespread use, remains an enigma to many. Whether you're a student, a professional, or someone looking to harness the power of data for personal projects, Excel is a pivotal ally in your quest. This book, "Excel Mastery: From Basics to Expert Visualisation Techniques," is designed to be your guide, teacher, and companion as you navigate the vast capabilities of Excel.

At its core, Excel is more than just a spreadsheet application; it's a powerful tool for data analysis, financial modelling, and decision-making. Its functions span from simple calculations to complex data manipulation, making it indispensable in today's data-driven world. The ability to effectively use Excel can enhance your job prospects, increase your efficiency, and provide you with insights that inform better decisions.

This book aims to demystify Excel for readers of all skill levels. Whether you're opening Excel for the first time or looking to refine your data visualisation skills, our goal is to present information in a clear, accessible manner. We understand that learning Excel can seem daunting, which is why we've broken down concepts into manageable chapters, each building on the last to ensure a comprehensive understanding.

You'll start with the basics, learning how to navigate the Excel interface and perform simple operations. From there, we'll delve into formulas, functions, and data organisation techniques, laying a solid foundation for more advanced topics. PivotTables, data analysis tools, and visualisation techniques will transform how you view and interpret data. By the end of this book, you'll not only be comfortable with Excel's most powerful features but also capable of creating insightful data reports and dashboards.

We encourage you to practise as you read. Excel is best learned by doing, so we've included exercises and examples to help solidify your understanding. Remember, mastery comes with patience and practice. No matter your starting point, this book is designed to guide you through to a level of proficiency where Excel becomes not just a tool, but a powerful extension of your analytical thinking.

Join us on this journey through Excel. By the end, you'll see data in a new light, armed with the knowledge and skills to analyse, visualise, and make informed decisions with confidence. Let's unlock the potential of Excel together.

Skipton Tech

What You Will Learn

This book is crafted to take you on a comprehensive journey through Microsoft Excel, transforming you from a novice to a confident user capable of handling sophisticated data analysis and visualisation tasks. Here's a snapshot of what awaits you:

1. **Understanding the Excel Interface**: You'll start with the basics, learning how to navigate Excel's interface with ease. This foundational knowledge will set the stage for everything that follows.

2. **Mastering Formulas and Functions**: Dive into the heart of Excel with an exploration of formulas and functions. From simple calculations to complex analytical tools, you'll learn how to manipulate data to uncover insights.

3. **Data Organisation Techniques**: Discover how to efficiently sort, filter, and organise your data. This skill is crucial for managing large datasets and preparing data for analysis.

4. **PivotTables and Data Analysis**: PivotTables are one of Excel's most powerful features. You'll learn how to summarise and analyse large datasets, making it easier to extract meaningful patterns and trends.

5. **Data Visualisation**: Transform your data into compelling visual stories. From basic charts to dynamic dashboards, you'll master the art of presenting data in visually engaging ways.

6. **Efficiency Boosters**: Uncover shortcuts and tips to enhance your productivity in Excel. These insights will save you time and streamline your workflow.

7. **Troubleshooting Common Problems**: Equip yourself with strategies to solve typical Excel challenges, ensuring a smoother experience as you work with your data.

How to Use This Book for Maximum Benefit

To get the most out of this book, consider the following tips:

Practice Regularly: Excel is best learned by doing. Try to replicate the examples provided, experiment with variations, and tackle the exercises at the end of each chapter.

Use the Chapter Progression: The book is designed with a logical progression in mind, from simple to complex topics. Even if you're familiar with some of the basics, reviewing them can provide new insights and strengthen your understanding.

Refer to the Appendices: The appendices include a list of functions, keyboard shortcuts, and additional resources. These can be valuable references as you practise and apply what you've learned.

Engage with the Exercises: The exercises are there to challenge and reinforce your learning. Don't skip them, even if they seem straightforward. They are an integral part of solidifying your Excel skills.

Be Patient and Persistent: Learning Excel is a marathon, not a sprint. Take your time with each concept, and don't be discouraged by mistakes, they're part of the learning process.

Keep Exploring: Once you've mastered the content of this book, don't stop there. Excel is constantly evolving, and there's always more to learn. Use what you've learned as a springboard to explore more advanced features and applications.

By following these guidelines, you'll not only learn Excel; you'll develop a valuable skill set that can enhance your career, academic pursuits, and personal projects. Let's embark on this learning adventure with enthusiasm and an open mind.

Chapter 1

Basic Formulas and Functions

Now that you're comfortable with entering data and navigating around Excel, let's explore one of its most powerful features: formulas and functions. These tools allow you to perform calculations and analyse your data efficiently.

Understanding Formulas:

A formula is an expression that calculates the value of a cell. For example, to add two numbers in Excel, you could enter `=1+2` into a cell. The equals sign (`=`) tells Excel that what follows is a formula. You can perform a variety of operations with formulas, such as addition (`+`), subtraction (`-`), multiplication (`*`), and division (`/`).

Creating a Simple Formula:

1. Click on the cell where you want the result of your calculation to appear.

2. Type `=` to start the formula, followed by the calculation you want to make. For instance, to add the values in cells A1 and B1, type `=A1+B1`.
3. Press Enter. Excel will calculate the result and display it in the cell.

Using Functions:

Functions are predefined formulas that make it easier to perform complex calculations. For example, the SUM function adds up all the numbers in a specific range of cells. To use a function:
1. Click on the cell where you want the result.
2. Type `=` followed by the function name and an open parenthesis. For example, to sum numbers in cells A1 through A5, type `=SUM(`.
3. Enter the range of cells you want to include in the calculation, like `A1:A5`.
4. Close the parenthesis and press Enter. Excel will perform the calculation and display the result.

Common Functions:

SUM: Adds up all the numbers in a range
(`=SUM(A1:A5)`).

AVERAGE: Calculates the average of numbers in a
range (`=AVERAGE(B1:B5)`).
MAX: Finds the highest number in a range
(`=MAX(C1:C5)`).
MIN: Finds the lowest number in a range
(`=MIN(D1:D5)`).

Copying Formulas and Functions:

When you've entered a formula or function into a
cell, you can copy it to other cells without retyping
the whole thing. This is particularly useful for
performing the same calculation across multiple
rows or columns.
1. Select the cell with the formula you want to copy.

2. Move your cursor to the bottom right corner of the cell until it changes to a small black cross (this is called the fill handle).
3. Click and drag the fill handle over the cells where you want to copy the formula. Excel will automatically adjust the formula for each cell.

Understanding Cell References:

When you copy formulas, Excel adjusts the cell references automatically. This is because most cell references are relative by default. For example, if you copy a formula from cell A1 to B1, Excel changes the reference from A1 to B1 automatically. If you want a cell reference to stay constant, use an absolute reference by adding a dollar sign (`$`) before the column letter and row number (`=$A$1`).

Formulas and functions are at the heart of Excel's data manipulation capabilities. By mastering these tools, you can start to unlock the true potential of your data. Practice creating formulas and using functions with different types of data to become more comfortable with these essential Excel skills.

Saving and Organising Excel Files

Managing your Excel files effectively is crucial for maintaining an efficient workflow and ensuring that your data is always accessible and secure. Here's how to save, organise, and manage your Excel workbooks.

Saving Your Workbook for the First Time:

1. **Using 'Save As'**: To save a new workbook, click on the File tab, then choose "Save As." You'll be prompted to select a location for your file (such as your computer or a cloud storage service) and to give it a name. Excel workbooks are typically saved with the `.xlsx` extension, but you can select other formats depending on your needs, such as `.xls` for compatibility with older versions of Excel or `.csv` for a comma-separated values file that can be used with many different programs.
2. **Choosing the Right Format**: Most of the time, you'll want to save your workbook in the default `.xlsx` format, which supports all Excel features. However, if you need to share your file with users who have older versions of Excel, consider saving a copy in the `.xls` format.

AutoSave Feature:

Excel's AutoSave feature can automatically save your workbooks to prevent data loss, especially when working on files stored in cloud services like OneDrive or SharePoint. Ensure AutoSave is enabled for critical documents to protect your progress.

Organising Your Excel Files:

Keeping your Excel files organised is key to working efficiently, especially as you accumulate more documents over time.

Use Folders: Create folders on your computer or cloud storage space for different projects, categories, or types of data. This makes it easier to find specific files when you need them.

Consistent Naming Conventions: Use clear and consistent naming conventions for your files and folders. Include dates, project names, or other identifiers that make the contents of the file clear at a glance.

Archiving: Periodically, review your folders for files that are no longer active and move them to an archive folder. This keeps your working folders uncluttered and ensures that only current files are in your immediate workspace.

Opening and Closing Workbooks:

Opening an Existing Workbook: To open a workbook you've previously saved, click on File > Open and navigate to the file's location. You can also quickly access recent files from the File menu.

Closing a Workbook: When you're done working with a workbook, you can close it by clicking on File

> Close. If there are unsaved changes, Excel will prompt you to save them before closing.

Backing Up Your Work:

Regularly backing up your Excel files is essential to avoid losing important data. Consider using cloud storage services that automatically backup your files, or set a schedule to manually back up your work to an external hard drive or another secure location.

By following these practices for saving, organising, and managing your Excel files, you'll ensure that your data is always safe, accessible, and easy to find. Remember, taking a little time to organise your files can save you a lot of time and trouble in the long run.

Chapter 2

Basic Formulas and Functions

Introduction to Formulas: Sum, Average, Min, Max

Formulas are the heart of Excel, allowing you to perform calculations and analyse your data. Let's start with some of the most basic and commonly used calculations: summing numbers, finding averages, and identifying minimum and maximum values.

Summing Numbers:

The `SUM` formula adds together a range of cells. For example, if you have numbers in cells A1 through A5 and you want to find their total, you would use the formula `=SUM(A1:A5)`. Simply type this into any cell and press Enter, and Excel will calculate the sum of those numbers.

Finding Averages:

The `AVERAGE` formula calculates the mean of a group of numbers. If you want to find the average of the same numbers in cells A1 through A5, use `=AVERAGE(A1:A5)`. This formula adds up all the numbers in the range and then divides by the count of those numbers to find the average.

Identifying Minimum and Maximum Values:

- The `MIN` formula helps you find the smallest number in a range. For instance, `=MIN(A1:A5)` will return the smallest number from cells A1 to A5.
- Conversely, the `MAX` formula gives you the largest number in a set. Typing `=MAX(A1:A5)` will reveal the highest value among the numbers in cells A1 through A5.

These basic formulas can be incredibly powerful when analysing data, allowing you to quickly get a sense of the totals, averages, extremes, and overall trends in your datasets.

Understanding Cell References: Relative, Absolute, and Mixed

When you're working with formulas in Excel, how you reference cells can significantly affect the outcome of your calculations. There are three main types of cell references: relative, absolute, and mixed.

Relative Cell References:

By default, cell references in Excel are relative. This means that when you copy a formula from one cell to another, the references in the formula adjust relative to the position of the new cell. For example, if you have a formula in cell B1 as `=A1+1` and you copy it to C1, the formula automatically changes to `=B1+1`. This is useful for applying the same operation across multiple cells.

Absolute Cell References:

Sometimes, you want a cell reference to stay fixed on a specific cell, even when you copy the formula elsewhere. You can achieve this by making the cell reference absolute. You do this by adding dollar signs before the column letter and row number, like `=$A$1`. If you have a formula `=$A$1+1` in cell B1 and copy it to C1, the formula will still reference A1, not change to B1.

Mixed references are a combination of relative and absolute references. You can fix either the column (e.g., `$A1`) or the row (e.g., `A$1`) or both. This is helpful when you need to keep one part of the reference constant while allowing the other part to adjust relative to where you copy the formula.

Basic Functions: COUNT, SUMIF, AVERAGEIF

In addition to the SUM, AVERAGE, MIN, and MAX functions, Excel offers a variety of functions to perform specific types of calculations. Here are three more basic but incredibly useful functions:

COUNT:

The `COUNT` function counts the number of cells in a range that contain numbers. For instance, `=COUNT(A1:A5)` will tell you how many of the cells from A1 to A5 have numbers in them.

SUMIF:

The `SUMIF` function adds up the values in a range that meet a specific criterion. Suppose you only want to sum the values in A1 through A5 that are greater than 10. You would use

`=SUMIF(A1:A5, ">10")`. This tells Excel to sum only the cells where the value is greater than 10.

AVERAGEIF:

Similarly, the `AVERAGEIF` function calculates the average of numbers in a range that meet a criterion. If you want the average of numbers in A1 through A5 but only for those greater than 10, use `=AVERAGEIF(A1:A5, ">10")`. This formula will only include the values greater than 10 in its calculation.

These functions expand your ability to analyse data, allowing you to perform targeted calculations based on specific conditions. By mastering these basic formulas and functions, you'll be well-equipped to start exploring more complex data analysis tasks in Excel.

Understanding Cell References: Relative, Absolute, and Mixed

Cell references are crucial in Excel because they tell your formulas where to look for the values or data they need to calculate. Let's delve deeper into understanding the differences between relative, absolute, and mixed cell references, and how you can use them effectively in your work.

Relative Cell References:

Relative cell references are the default type in Excel. When you copy a formula that includes a relative reference from one cell to another, Excel automatically adjusts the reference based on the formula's new location. This is incredibly useful for applying the same formula across multiple cells or rows efficiently.

Example: If you have a formula `=A1+B1` in cell C1 and you copy it to C2, the formula automatically adjusts to `=A2+B2`. This happens because Excel updates the references to match the new row, keeping the formula relative to its position.

Absolute Cell References:

Absolute cell references, on the other hand, remain constant, no matter where you copy your formula. This is achieved by placing a dollar sign (`$`) before the column letter and row number in your cell reference. Absolute references are essential when you need a formula to refer back to a specific cell, regardless of where the formula is located in the worksheet.

Example: If you want to multiply a series of numbers by a single constant value located in A1, you would use a formula like `=B1*$A$1` in cell C1.

If you copy this formula down column C, the reference to cell A1 remains constant in every formula.

Mixed Cell References:

Mixed cell references combine relative and absolute references. You can lock either the column or the row (but not both), allowing the other part of the reference to adjust relatively when the formula is copied. This type is particularly useful in more complex spreadsheets where you might want to keep one dimension constant while allowing the other to change.

Example: If you have a formula `=A1*$B$1` in cell C1 and you copy it to D1, the reference to B1 stays absolute, but A1 changes to B1 because the column changes while the row remains the same. If you were to copy C1 to C2 instead, A1 would change to A2 (since it's a row change and the column reference is relative), but B1 would remain fixed.

How to Use Them:

- Use **relative references** when you need your formulas to adjust automatically as you fill them across rows or columns.

- Use **absolute references** when you need to refer to a specific cell that contains a constant value or parameter, no matter where in your sheet.
- Use **mixed references** when you need a combination of both behaviours for more complex calculations and data arrangements.

Understanding and applying these types of cell references correctly can significantly enhance your ability to build flexible and powerful Excel models. It allows you to create dynamic formulas that can be easily replicated across your workbook, saving time and reducing errors in your data analysis.

Next, we'll explore some basic but powerful functions that are essential for data analysis: COUNT, SUMIF, and AVERAGEIF, and how they can be used to perform calculations based on specific criteria.

Basic Functions: COUNT, SUMIF, AVERAGEIF

Expanding your toolkit with Excel's basic functions can significantly streamline your data analysis process. Let's explore three more functions that are invaluable for managing and interpreting your data: COUNT, SUMIF, and AVERAGEIF. These functions help you count cells, sum values based on a condition, and calculate an average based on a condition, respectively.

COUNT:

The COUNT function is used to count the number of cells that contain numbers in a specified range. It's incredibly useful for quickly assessing how many entries in a dataset are numeric, which is a common need in data analysis.

Syntax: `=COUNT(range)`
Example: If you want to count how many cells in the range A1:A10 contain numbers, you would use `=COUNT(A1:A10)`.

SUMIF:

The SUMIF function sums up the values in a range that meet a specified criterion. This function is particularly handy when you need to sum values under certain conditions, such as adding up sales in a specific region or totaling expenses of a certain type.

Syntax: `=SUMIF(range, criteria, [sum_range])`
   range: The range of cells you want evaluated by your criteria.
   criteria: The condition that determines which cells to sum.

sum_range: The actual cells to sum. If omitted, Excel sums the cells in the range.

Example: To sum all values in B1:B10 that are greater than 50, you would use `=SUMIF(B1:B10, ">50")`. If you wanted to sum corresponding values in C1:C10 based on criteria applied to B1:B10, you would use `=SUMIF(B1:B10, ">50", C1:C10)`.

AVERAGEIF:

Similar to SUMIF, the AVERAGEIF function calculates the average of numbers in a range that meet a specified criterion. It's useful for finding the average value under specific conditions, such as the average sales amount for a particular product or the average score from a group of tests.

Syntax: `=AVERAGEIF(range, criteria, [average_range])`

range: The range of cells you want evaluated by your criteria.

criteria: The condition that determines which cells to consider for the average.

average_range: The actual cells to average. If omitted, Excel averages the cells in the range.

Example: If you want to calculate the average of numbers in B1:B10 that are greater than 20, you would use `=AVERAGEIF(B1:B10, ">20")`. To find the average of corresponding values in C1:C10 based on criteria applied to B1:B10, use `=AVERAGEIF(B1:B10, ">20", C1:C10)`.

Practical Applications:
- Use **COUNT** to quickly determine how many entries in a list are numeric, helping you understand the dataset's composition.
- Apply **SUMIF** to perform conditional sums, such as adding up expenses in a certain category or totaling sales in a specific region.
- Utilise **AVERAGEIF** to calculate conditional averages, which can reveal underlying trends or insights, such as the average transaction size for sales over a certain amount or the average score for students who passed an exam.

Mastering these functions allows you to perform a wide range of data analysis tasks more efficiently. By incorporating COUNT, SUMIF, and AVERAGEIF into your Excel skill set, you can analyse your data with greater precision and uncover insights that inform better decision-making. Remember, practice is key to becoming proficient, so try applying these functions to your data to see how they can improve your analysis workflow.

Chapter 3

Logical Functions

Logical functions in Excel are incredibly useful for making decisions with your data based on specific criteria. They allow you to perform different actions depending on whether certain conditions are met. In this chapter, we'll explore how to use the IF, AND, OR functions for decision-making, as well as delve into nested IFs and combining IF with other functions.

Using IF, AND, OR Functions for Decision-Making

IF Function:

The IF function is one of the most popular logical functions in Excel. It checks whether a condition is met, returns one value if the condition is true, and another value if it's false.

Syntax: `=IF(condition, value_if_true, value_if_false)`

Example: Suppose you want to check if a number in cell A1 is greater than 10. If it is, you want to display "Yes"; if not, display "No". The formula would be `=IF(A1>10, "Yes", "No")`.

AND Function:

The AND function checks if all conditions in a test are true. It's often used inside an IF function to test multiple conditions at once.

Syntax: `=AND(condition1, condition2, ...)`
Example: If you want to check whether a number in cell A1 is greater than 10 and less than 20, you could use `=IF(AND(A1>10, A1<20), "Yes", "No")`. This formula returns "Yes" only if both conditions are met.

OR Function:

The OR function checks if any of the conditions in a test are true. Like AND, it's commonly used with IF to allow for multiple possible true conditions.

Syntax: `=OR(condition1, condition2, ...)`
Example: To check if a number in cell A1 is either less than 10 or greater than 20, you would use `=IF(OR(A1<10, A1>20), "Yes", "No")`. This formula returns "Yes" if either condition is true.

Nested IFs and Using IF with Other Functions

Nested IFs:

Sometimes, you might need to check multiple conditions that require more than a simple true or false outcome. In such cases, you can use nested IF statements, which means using one IF function inside another.

Example: If you want to categorise a score in cell A1 (where a score less than 50 is "Fail", between 50 and 70 is "Pass", and above 70 is "Excellent"), you could use a nested IF: `=IF(A1<50, "Fail", IF(A1<=70, "Pass", "Excellent"))`. This formula first checks if the score is less than 50. If not, it moves to the next IF function to see if the score is less than or equal to 70, and so on.

Using IF with Other Functions:

Combining IF with other functions can make your formulas even more powerful. For example, you can use IF with the SUM, AVERAGE, or COUNT functions to perform calculations only if certain conditions are met.

Example: To calculate the average of numbers in the range A1:A10 only if the sum of those numbers is greater than 100, you could use: `=IF(SUM(A1:A10)>100, AVERAGE(A1:A10), "Total is too low")`. This checks if the sum of A1:A10 is greater than 100, and if so, it calculates the average; if not, it displays a message.

Logical functions like IF, AND, and OR open up a world of possibilities for analysing your data based on conditions. By mastering these functions, you can create more dynamic and responsive spreadsheets that automatically adapt based on the data they contain. Practice applying these functions to your data sets to see how they can enhance your decision-making processes in Excel.

Nested IFs and Using IF with Other Functions

Expanding upon the foundational knowledge of logical functions, let's delve deeper into the practical applications of nested IF statements and the integration of the IF function with other Excel functions to create more sophisticated and dynamic analyses.

Nested IFs for Multiple Conditions:

When you have more than two conditions to evaluate, nested IFs become invaluable. A nested IF means placing an IF function inside another IF function, allowing for multiple outcomes.

Syntax for Nested IF: `=IF(condition1, value_if_true1, IF(condition2, value_if_true2, value_if_false2))`

Example: Imagine you're grading tests with the following criteria: scores over 80 are graded as "A", scores between 60 and 80 are "B", scores between 40 and 60 are "C", and scores below 40 are "D". The formula for this might look like `=IF(A1>80, "A", IF(A1>60, "B", IF(A1>40, "C", "D")))`. Here, Excel evaluates each condition in turn, moving to the next IF statement if the previous condition is false.

Combining IF with AND/OR:

To evaluate multiple conditions within a single IF function, you can combine IF with AND or OR functions for more complex decision-making.

Using IF with AND: `=IF(AND(condition1, condition2), value_if_true, value_if_false)`

Example: To determine if a student passes where the conditions are a score above 50 and attendance above 75%, `=IF(AND(B1>50, C1>75), "Pass", "Fail")`.

Using IF with OR: `=IF(OR(condition1, condition2), value_if_true, value_if_false)`

Example: To check if a student is eligible for a retake given either a score below 50 or attendance below 75%, `=IF(OR(B1<50, C1<75), "Eligible for Retake", "Not Eligible")`.

Using IF with Other Functions:

The power of IF is not just limited to logical tests; it can be combined with various other functions to perform conditional calculations.

Example with SUMIF: Suppose you want to sum only the sales that exceed $1000. You could use `=SUMIF(B2:B10, ">1000")`. But to provide a conditional message or calculation, you might say `=IF(SUMIF(B2:B10, ">1000")>5000, "Target Exceeded", "Target Not Met")`, combining SUMIF with an IF condition to give feedback based on the sum result.

Example with AVERAGE and COUNTIF: To calculate the average sales only if there are more than 5 sales records that exceed $1000, you could use `=IF(COUNTIF(B2:B10, ">1000")>5, AVERAGE(B2:B10), "Not Enough Data")`. This formula first counts how many sales exceed $1000 and then calculates the average only if there are more than 5 such sales.

Tips for Working with Nested IFs and Complex Formulas:

Clarity: Nested IFs can become complex and hard to read. Use comments in your formulas (by adding a note in the cell) to explain the logic for future reference.

Alternative Functions: For complex criteria, consider using the `IFS` function (available in Excel 2019 and later), which can simplify nested IF statements by evaluating multiple conditions without nesting.

Error Checking: Use Excel's formula auditing tools to trace and debug complex nested IF formulas, ensuring they work as intended.

By mastering nested IFs and learning to combine IF with other functions, you can significantly enhance your data analysis capabilities in Excel. These techniques allow for nuanced decision-making and analysis, tailored to the specific needs of your datasets. Practise these concepts with real-world data to build your confidence and proficiency.

Chapter 4

Lookup Functions

Lookup functions in Excel are incredibly powerful tools that allow you to search for data within a table or range and return a value from a specific position. This chapter introduces you to the basics of VLOOKUP and HLOOKUP, two of the most commonly used lookup functions, followed by an introduction to the more flexible and powerful combination of INDEX and MATCH.

VLOOKUP and HLOOKUP Basics

VLOOKUP Basics:

VLOOKUP stands for Vertical Lookup. It is used to search for a value in the first column of a table and return a value in the same row from a specified column.

Syntax: `=VLOOKUP(lookup_value, table_array, col_index_num, [range_lookup])`
   lookup_value: The value you want to search for.
   table_array: The range of cells that contains the data.

col_index_num: The column number in the table from which to retrieve the value.

range_lookup: Optional. TRUE for an approximate match, or FALSE for an exact match.

Example: Suppose you have a list of products and prices in columns A and B, respectively. To find the price of a product named "Widget" listed in cell A2, you could use `=VLOOKUP("Widget", A2:B10, 2, FALSE)`. This formula searches for "Widget" in the first column of A2:B10 and returns the value from the second column in the same row.

HLOOKUP Basics:

HLOOKUP stands for Horizontal Lookup. It works similarly to VLOOKUP but searches for a value in the first row of a table and returns a value in the same column from a specified row.

Syntax: `=HLOOKUP(lookup_value, table_array, row_index_num, [range_lookup])`

lookup_value: The value to search for.

table_array: The range of cells containing the data.

row_index_num: The row number in the table from which to retrieve the value.

range_lookup: Optional. TRUE for an approximate match, or FALSE for an exact match.

Example: If you have a table where months are listed in the first row and sales data is listed in rows below, to find the sales for "March" in the second row, you could use `=HLOOKUP("March", A1:G2, 2, FALSE)`. This searches for "March" in the first row of A1:G2 and returns the value from the second row.

Introduction to INDEX and MATCH for Flexible Lookups

While VLOOKUP and HLOOKUP are straightforward and useful, they have limitations, such as the inability to look to the left of the lookup value with VLOOKUP or above the lookup value with HLOOKUP. This is where the combination of INDEX and MATCH functions becomes a game-changer, offering greater flexibility and accuracy in lookups.

INDEX Function:

The INDEX function returns a value or the reference to a value from within a table or range.

Syntax: `=INDEX(array, row_num, [column_num])`
   array: The range of cells that contains the data.
   row_num: The row number in the array from which to retrieve the value.
   column_num: Optional. The column number in the array from which to retrieve the value.

MATCH Function:

The MATCH function searches for a specified item in a range of cells and then returns the relative position of that item.

Syntax: `=MATCH(lookup_value, lookup_array, [match_type])`
    lookup_value: The value you want to search for.
    lookup_array: The range of cells containing possible lookup values.
    match_type: Optional. 1 for less than, 0 for exact match, -1 for greater than.

Combining INDEX and MATCH:

By combining these two functions, you can perform lookups in any direction—left, right, up, and down—within a table.

Syntax for a combined formula: `=INDEX(array, MATCH(lookup_value, lookup_array, 0))`
Example: To find the price of a product named "Widget" in a table where the product names are in column A and the prices are in column B, use `=INDEX(B1:B10, MATCH("Widget", A1:A10, 0))`. This formula first finds the position of "Widget" in the range A1:A10 using MATCH, then returns the value from the same position in the range B1:B10 using INDEX.

The combination of INDEX and MATCH is more powerful and versatile than VLOOKUP and HLOOKUP because it allows for two-way lookups, provides the ability to search for values in any column or row, and avoids some of the limitations associated with V

LOOKUP and HLOOKUP. Mastering these functions can significantly enhance your data analysis capabilities in Excel, making it easier to find and work with the information you need.

Chapter 5

Date and Time Functions

Excel is not just powerful for numerical data analysis; it also offers robust support for working with dates and times. Understanding how to manipulate and calculate dates and times can help you track project timelines, measure durations, and schedule future events efficiently. This chapter covers some of the essential date and time functions in Excel, including TODAY, NOW, DATE, and DATEDIF.

Working with Dates and Times: TODAY, NOW, DATE, DATEDIF

TODAY Function:

The TODAY function returns the current date. It doesn't require any arguments and automatically updates each day when you open your workbook.

Syntax: `=TODAY()`
Example: To display today's date in a cell, simply enter `=TODAY()`. This can be useful for tracking

current deadlines or as a reference point in calculations involving the current date.

NOW Function:

The NOW function returns the current date and time. Like TODAY, it updates automatically and is useful for timestamping or calculations involving the exact time.

Syntax: `=NOW()`
Example: To insert the current date and time into a cell, use `=NOW()`. This function can be particularly useful for logging specific events or tracking time-sensitive tasks.

DATE Function:

The DATE function allows you to create a date based on individual year, month, and day components. It's particularly useful for constructing dates dynamically from other data in your workbook.

Syntax: `=DATE(year, month, day)`
Example: To create a date representing March 15, 2023, you would use `=DATE(2023, 3, 15)`. This can help in creating custom dates for project planning, scheduling, and historical data analysis.

DATEDIF Function:

The DATEDIF function calculates the difference between two dates. It's a versatile function that can return the difference in days, months, or years, depending on the unit specified.

Syntax: `=DATEDIF(start_date, end_date, "unit")`
  start_date: The starting date of the period.
  end_date: The ending date of the period.
  unit: The unit of time to calculate. Use "D" for days, "M" for months, and "Y" for years.
Example: To find out how many days are between January 1, 2023, and March 31, 2023, use `=DATEDIF("1/1/2023", "3/31/2023", "D")`. This function is incredibly useful for tracking durations, calculating ages, or measuring periods between events.

Calculating Differences Between Dates, Working with Workdays

Calculating the difference between two dates is a common task in Excel, whether for project timelines, billing cycles, or event planning. Beyond DATEDIF, Excel provides functions to calculate workdays, which exclude weekends and optionally holidays.

NETWORKDAYS Function:

The NETWORKDAYS function calculates the number of workdays between two dates, automatically excluding weekends (Saturday and Sunday) and optionally a list of holidays.

Syntax: `=NETWORKDAYS(start_date, end_date, [holidays])`
    start_date: The start date of the period.
    end_date: The end date of the period.
    holidays: Optional. A range that contains dates to be excluded from the workday count as holidays.
Example: To calculate the number of workdays from January 1, 2023, to March 31, 2023, excluding New Year's Day and Martin Luther King Jr. Day, you could use `=NETWORKDAYS("1/1/2023", "3/31/2023", B1:B2)` assuming B1:B2 contains the holiday dates. This function is essential for project planning and tracking workday-based durations.

Understanding and utilising Excel's date and time functions can significantly enhance your data management and analysis capabilities. From simply tracking the current date and time to complex calculations involving periods and workdays, these functions provide the tools you need to handle temporal data effectively. Practice with these functions to become more proficient in scheduling, planning, and time-based data analysis.

Calculating Differences Between Dates, Working with Workdays

Beyond the basics of date and time functions like TODAY and DATEDIF, Excel provides specialised functions for dealing with workdays and calculating differences between dates that factor in working days only. This is especially useful in project management, HR, and any field where business days are the standard measurement of time.

NETWORKDAYS Function:

NETWORKDAYS calculates the number of whole working days between two dates, automatically excluding weekends (Saturday and Sunday) and any dates identified as holidays.

Syntax: `=NETWORKDAYS(start_date, end_date, [holidays])`
   start_date: The start date from which to begin the count.
   end_date: The end date at which to stop the count.
   holidays: Optional. A range of dates that should be excluded from the count of working days, such as public holidays.
Example: To calculate the number of workdays between January 1, 2024, and January 31, 2024, excluding January 1st as a holiday, you would use:

`=NETWORKDAYS("1/1/2024", "1/31/2024", "1/1/2024")`. This formula will return the number of weekdays in January, minus New Year's Day.

NETWORKDAYS.INTL Function:

For a more global application, NETWORKDAYS.INTL allows customisation of which days are considered weekends. This is particularly useful in countries where the weekend might not fall on Saturday and Sunday.

Syntax: `=NETWORKDAYS.INTL(start_date, end_date, [weekend], [holidays])`
   weekend: Optional. A number or string specifying which days of the week are considered weekends.
   holidays: Optional. A range specifying any dates that should be excluded from the count of workdays.
Example: If you're working in a region where Friday and Saturday are the weekend, to calculate workdays in January while excluding a specific holiday, you might use:
`=NETWORKDAYS.INTL("1/1/2024", "1/31/2024", "7", A1:A2)`, where "7" indicates Friday and Saturday as weekends, and A1:A2 contains the holiday dates.

WORKDAY Function:

The WORKDAY function is used to calculate a date a specified number of workdays before or after a start date, excluding weekends and optionally holidays. This is useful for project planning and deadline tracking.

Syntax: `=WORKDAY(start_date, days, [holidays])`
   days: The number of workdays before (negative value) or after (positive value) the start date.
   holidays: Optional. A range of dates that are to be excluded from the count as holidays.
Example: To find the date 10 workdays after January 1, 2024, while excluding holidays listed in range A1:A2, use: `=WORKDAY("1/1/2024", 10, A1:A2)`. This function will give you the exact date after accounting for weekends and holidays.

WORKDAY.INTL Function:

Similar to NETWORKDAYS.INTL, WORKDAY.INTL allows for customization of which days are considered weekends. This function is ideal for calculating future or past dates based on a custom workweek.

Syntax: `=WORKDAY.INTL(start_date, days, [weekend], [holidays])`
   weekend: Optional. A number or string that defines the days of the week that are weekends.

holidays: Optional. A range of dates to exclude from the calculation as holidays.
Example: To find the date 15 work days from January 1, 2024, considering Friday and Saturday as weekends and excluding specific holidays, you might use: `=WORKDAY.INTL("1/1/2024", 15, "7", A1:A2)`.

By utilising these functions, you can accurately calculate durations and deadlines that align with work schedules, taking into account weekends and holidays. This capability is invaluable for project management, allowing for precise scheduling and planning. Practice using these functions with your data to become proficient in managing timelines and schedules in Excel.

Chapter 6

Data Organisation

Organising your data effectively is crucial in Excel to ensure that you can analyse and find information quickly and efficiently. This chapter focuses on two key aspects of data organisation: sorting and filtering data, and implementing data validation for input control.

Sorting and Filtering Data

Sorting Data:

Sorting your data helps you arrange it in a meaningful order, such as alphabetically, numerically, or by date, which can make it easier to analyse.

Basic Sorting:
   - To sort data, first select the column or range you want to organise.
   - Use the "Sort A to Z" or "Sort Z to A" buttons on the Data tab for quick sorting.

- For numbers, this will sort from smallest to largest or vice versa. For dates, from earliest to latest or the opposite.

Advanced Sorting:
- For more control, use the "Sort" dialog box on the Data tab.
- Here, you can sort by multiple columns. For example, you could first sort by department and then by employee name within each department.

Filtering Data:

Filtering allows you to view only the rows that meet certain criteria, hiding the rest. This is useful when you're looking for specific information in a large dataset.

Applying Filters:
- Click on the "Filter" button on the Data tab to add dropdown arrows to each column header in your data range.
- Click these arrows to see filtering options, such as checking off which items to display, choosing to filter by specific criteria, or using number filters to show rows that meet certain numerical conditions.

Data Validation for Input Control

Data validation is a feature that restricts the type of data or the values that users can enter into a cell. This is especially useful for maintaining accuracy and consistency in your datasets.

Setting Up Data Validation:

- Select the cell or range where you want to apply validation.
- Go to the Data tab and click on "Data Validation."
- In the dialog box, you can choose the type of data allowed (e.g., date, number, list), and then specify further, such as setting a minimum and maximum value for numbers.

Creating Drop-Down Lists:

- One common use of data validation is creating a drop-down list.
- In the "Data Validation" dialog box, select "List" under "Allow," and then enter the list of values either directly in the "Source" box or reference a range on the worksheet where your list is located.
- This ensures that entries in a cell come only from a predefined set of options, reducing the chance of errors.

Input Messages and Error Alerts:

- You can also set input messages that appear when the cell is selected, guiding users on what to enter.

- If a user tries to enter something that doesn't fit the validation criteria, Excel can display an error alert. You can customise this message to make it clear what kind of data is expected.

Practical Applications:

Sorting and Filtering: These tools are invaluable for managing large tables of data, such as sales records, inventory lists, or schedules. By organising your data, you can more easily identify trends, outliers, or specific items of interest.

Data Validation: Use data validation to ensure data integrity in forms, surveys, or any spreadsheet where data consistency is crucial. For example, you can ensure that all entries In a "Date of Birth" column are actual dates or that values in a "Sales Amount" column are within a reasonable range.

Mastering sorting, filtering, and data validation will significantly enhance your ability to manage and analyse data in Excel. These features not only help keep your data organised and accessible but also safeguard against common data entry errors, making your spreadsheets more reliable and easier to use.

Chapter 7

PivotTables

PivotTables are one of Excel's most powerful features, allowing you to summarise, analyse, explore, and present your data. PivotTables make it easy to transform extensive and complex datasets into meaningful reports and charts. This chapter will guide you through creating PivotTables for data summaries, customising them with grouping and calculated fields, and enhancing your data analysis with slicers and timelines for interactive filtering.

Creating PivotTables for Data Summary

What is a PivotTable?

A PivotTable is an Excel tool that allows you to reorganise and summarise selected columns and rows of data in a spreadsheet to obtain a desired report.

Steps to Create a PivotTable:

1. **Select Your Data**: First, highlight the range of data you want to analyse with your PivotTable. This data should be organised in a table format with clear column headings.

2. **Insert a PivotTable**: Go to the Insert tab on the Ribbon and click on the PivotTable button. Excel will ask you to confirm the data range you're using and whether you want the PivotTable to be placed in a new worksheet or an existing one.

3. **Choose Fields for Your PivotTable**: In the PivotTable Field List pane, drag and drop the fields you want to analyse into the Report Filter, Column Labels, Row Labels, and Values areas. Excel will automatically generate a summary based on your selection.

    Row Labels are used for the data you want to list down the page.

    Column Labels are used for the data you want to spread across the page.

    Values are the data that will be summarised and calculated based on the row and column labels.

    Report Filter allows you to filter the entire PivotTable based on a particular aspect.

Customising PivotTables: Grouping, Calculated Fields

Grouping Data:

PivotTables allow you to group your data by specific values, dates, or custom groupings, providing more detailed insights.

Example: If you have a date field in your PivotTable, you can group by month, quarter, or year to analyse data over time.

Adding Calculated Fields:

You can enhance your PivotTable by adding calculated fields, which are formulas that use the sum of other data fields in the PivotTable.

Steps to Add a Calculated Field: Choose the PivotTable Analyze tab → Fields, Items, & Sets → Calculated Field. Enter a name for your calculated field, write the formula, and click OK.

Slicers and Timelines for Interactive Filtering

Slicers:

Slicers are visual filters. While traditional filters hide rows or columns of data that do not meet certain criteria, slicers make it easy to filter the PivotTable data visually. They are particularly useful because they provide a clear indication of what data is being displayed.

How to Add a Slicer: Click anywhere inside your PivotTable, go to the PivotTable Analyze tab, and select Insert Slicer. Choose the field(s) you want to use as a filter, and click OK. You can then click the options in the slicer to filter your PivotTable data.

Timelines:

Timelines are similar to slicers but are specifically used for filtering dates. They provide a graphical way to filter PivotTable data over time, making it straightforward to select ranges of dates with a slider control.

How to Add a Timeline: Ensure your PivotTable has a date field. Click anywhere in your PivotTable, go to the PivotTable Analyze tab, and select Insert

Timeline. Choose the date field you want to use, and click OK. You can now use the timeline to filter your data by selecting time periods.

By mastering PivotTables, you unlock a dynamic way to present and analyse your data in Excel. From summarising vast datasets to filtering data for specific insights, PivotTables and their customisation features like grouping, calculated fields, slicers, and timelines empower you to draw meaningful conclusions from your data efficiently. Practice creating and customising PivotTables with your datasets to become proficient in these powerful Excel functionalities.

Customising PivotTables: Grouping, Calculated Fields

After you've created a PivotTable, you may want to dive deeper into your data analysis by customising your PivotTable to show exactly the insights you need. Let's explore how to enhance your PivotTables through grouping and adding calculated fields.

Grouping Data in PivotTables:

Grouping allows you to combine data into categories, making it easier to analyse subsets of your data.

Grouping by Dates: Right-click on a date in your PivotTable, select "Group," and then choose the time period for grouping, such as months, quarters, or years. This feature is handy for analysing trends over time.

Grouping Numbers: You can group numerical data to analyse it in ranges. Right-click on a number within your PivotTable, select "Group," and then specify the starting and ending points, along with the interval for each group.

Grouping Text: While Excel doesn't allow direct text grouping in the PivotTable field list, you can manually group items by selecting them and then right-clicking to choose "Group." This can be useful for categorising similar items under a common name.

Adding Calculated Fields to PivotTables:

Calculated fields let you perform calculations on other fields in the PivotTable. For example, you can create a calculated field to analyse profit margins or percentage growth.

Creating a Calculated Field: Click anywhere in your PivotTable to activate the PivotTable Tools on the ribbon. Go to the Analyze tab, click on "Fields, Items, & Sets," and select "Calculated Field." Enter a name for your field, construct the formula, and then click "OK." Your calculated field will now appear as part of your PivotTable.

Slicers and Timelines for Interactive Filtering

Enhancing your PivotTables with slicers and timelines not only makes your data more interactive but also enables users to filter and analyse data dynamically.

Using Slicers for Easy Filtering:

Slicers provide a quick way to filter PivotTable data visually. They are especially useful in dashboards and reports where non-technical users need to interact with the data.

Adding a Slicer: With your PivotTable selected, go to the PivotTable Analyze tab and click "Insert Slicer." Choose the fields for which you want to create slicers. Once added, you can click on the slicer buttons to filter your PivotTable data based on those fields.

Customising Slicers: You can customise the appearance of slicers by selecting them and using the options under the Slicer Tools -> Options tab on the ribbon. You can change the slicer's colour, number of columns, and button styles to match your report's design.

Implementing Timelines for Date Filtering:

Timelines are an intuitive way to filter PivotTable data by date. They are particularly useful for reports that need dynamic time-based analysis.

Adding a Timeline: With your PivotTable active, go to the PivotTable Analyze tab and click "Insert Timeline." Choose the date field you wish to filter by. The timeline will appear, allowing you to select date ranges via a sliding bar.

Customising Timelines: Like slicers, timelines can be customised to fit the look and feel of your reports. You can adjust their size, style, and the time periods displayed for easy navigation through your data.

By customising your PivotTables with grouping, calculated fields, slicers, and timelines, you significantly enhance the interactivity and analytical power of your Excel reports. These tools not only make your data more accessible but also allow for deeper insights and more dynamic data exploration. Practice incorporating these features into your PivotTables to unlock the full potential of your data analysis in Excel.

Slicers and Timelines for Interactive Filtering

Slicers and timelines enhance your PivotTables and PivotCharts by providing a user-friendly interface for filtering data. These features allow users to quickly refine and analyse datasets, making your Excel reports interactive and more accessible.

Slicers for Categorical Data Filtering

Slicers offer a visual way to filter data based on categories. Unlike traditional filters that hide within drop-down menus at the top of columns, slicers are displayed on the spreadsheet, allowing for easy access and interaction.

How to Add Slicers:
1. Click inside your PivotTable.
2. Navigate to the PivotTable Analyze tab and select "Insert Slicer."
3. In the dialog box, check the boxes for the fields you want to add slicers for, and click OK.

4. You'll see the slicers appear as boxes with buttons for each category in the field.

Customising Slicers:

Slicers can be customised to fit the theme and style of your report. You can change the colour, size, and number of columns of buttons within the slicer to make it more user-friendly. Simply click on a slicer to activate the Slicer Tools in the Ribbon, where you will find options to customise your slicer's appearance.

Connecting Slicers to Multiple PivotTables:

A powerful feature of slicers is their ability to control multiple PivotTables simultaneously. If you have several PivotTables derived from the same data source, you can connect a slicer to all of them, ensuring that when you filter on the slicer, all connected PivotTables update to reflect the filter.

Timelines for Time-Based Data Filtering

Timelines are specifically designed for filtering dates in PivotTables, providing a graphical slider interface. They are particularly useful for reports that require dynamic time-based analysis.

How to Add Timelines:

1. Ensure your PivotTable includes a field with date information.
2. Click anywhere inside your PivotTable.
3. Go to the PivotTable Analyze tab and click "Insert Timeline."
4. Select the date field you wish to create a timeline for and click OK.
5. A timeline will appear, allowing you to select time periods by dragging the edges of the slider or clicking on specific time periods.

Customising Timelines:

Like slicers, timelines can be customised to better match your report's layout and style. Once you select a timeline, the Timeline Tools will appear in the Ribbon, offering options to change the timeline's style, period labels, and overall appearance.

Benefits of Using Slicers and Timelines:

Enhanced Interactivity: Slicers and timelines make your data reports interactive, allowing end-users to explore and drill down into the data based on their interests.

Improved Accessibility: With slicers and timelines, filtering data becomes more intuitive, eliminating the need to navigate complex menus.

Consistency Across Reports: Connecting slicers and timelines to multiple PivotTables ensures consistent data views across your entire report, enhancing the cohesiveness and accuracy of your analysis.

Incorporating slicers and timelines into your PivotTables not only enriches the analytical experience but also significantly increases the usability and interactivity of your Excel reports. By enabling dynamic, user-driven data exploration, you empower report viewers to discover insights that static tables and charts might not readily reveal. Practice adding, customising, and connecting slicers and timelines to your PivotTables to master these powerful Excel features.

Chapter 8

Advanced Functions and Formulas

As you become more comfortable with Excel, you may encounter situations that require more sophisticated analyses. This chapter introduces advanced functions and formulas that can handle complex calculations, including array formulas, the SUMPRODUCT function, and dynamic named ranges. These tools can significantly enhance your ability to work with and analyse data in Excel.

Array Formulas for Complex Calculations

Array Formulas:

Array formulas can perform multiple calculations on one or more items in an array, returning either a single result or multiple results. Array formulas are powerful because they allow you to do things that might not be possible with standard formulas.

How to Use Array Formulas:

To create an array formula, you enter the formula into a cell, then press Ctrl+Shift+Enter (CSE) instead of just Enter. This tells Excel that you're entering an array formula, allowing it to process the formula differently. Excel will surround your formula with curly braces `{}`; however, you do not type these.

Example of an Array Formula:
Suppose you have a list of sales in column A and a list of costs in column B. To calculate the total profit for all items, you could use the array formula `=SUM(A1:A10-B1:B10)`. After typing the formula, press Ctrl+Shift+Enter, and Excel will calculate the profit for each item and then sum those profits to give you a total.

Using SUMPRODUCT for Multi-Condition Sums

SUMPRODUCT Function:

The SUMPRODUCT function multiplies corresponding components in the given arrays and returns the sum of those products. It's incredibly versatile and can be used for tasks such as conditional sums across multiple criteria without the complexity of array formulas.

Syntax and Use:

The basic syntax for SUMPRODUCT is
`=SUMPRODUCT(array1, [array2], [array3], ...)`.
Each array could be a range of cells or an array
constant.

Example of SUMPRODUCT:

If you want to calculate the total sales only for a
specific product type and within a specific region,
you could use SUMPRODUCT. Assume product
types are listed in column A, regions in column B,
sales in column C, and you're interested in "Widget"
sales in the "North" region. The formula could be
`=SUMPRODUCT((A1:A10="Widget")*(B1:B10="N
orth"), C1:C10)`. This formula checks each row to
see if it matches both conditions and then sums the
sales amounts that do.

Dynamic Named Ranges for
Flexible Formulas

Dynamic Named Ranges:

A dynamic named range expands automatically to
include new data as it's added. This is useful for
creating charts that update dynamically or for

formulas that need to consider an entire dataset that may grow or shrink.

Creating a Dynamic Named Range:

You can create a dynamic named range using the Name Manager and Excel's OFFSET function combined with the COUNTA function for non-blank cells or the COUNT function for numerical cells.

Example of Creating a Dynamic Named Range:

Suppose you have a list of sales figures in column A that will grow over time. You can create a dynamic named range called "SalesData" using the formula `=OFFSET($A$1,0,0,COUNTA($A:$A),1)`. This formula creates a range starting at A1, which expands down as many rows as there are non-blank cells in column A but stays one column wide.

By integrating these advanced functions and formulas into your Excel workbooks, you can handle a wider range of data analysis tasks more efficiently. Array formulas allow for complex calculations across multiple data points, SUMPRODUCT offers a powerful tool for conditional analysis, and dynamic named ranges ensure your formulas always work with the most current data. Experimenting with these advanced features will enhance your Excel skills and enable you to tackle more sophisticated data analysis challenges.

Using SUMPRODUCT for Multi-Condition Sums

The **SUMPRODUCT** function is a versatile tool in Excel that performs array operations on ranges of cells. It's particularly useful for conducting multi-condition sums without needing to resort to complex array formulas. SUMPRODUCT can evaluate conditions and perform calculations, making it an essential function for data analysis tasks that involve multiple criteria.

Syntax and Use:

The syntax for SUMPRODUCT is `=SUMPRODUCT(array1, [array2], [array3], ...)`. Each array argument must have the same length; SUMPRODUCT multiplies the elements of the arrays positionally and then sums these products.

Practical Example:
Imagine you have a dataset where column A lists product names, column B lists regions, and column C contains sales figures. You want to calculate the total sales for a specific product within a specific

region. Using SUMPRODUCT, you can multiply a series of TRUE/FALSE conditions (converted to 1s and 0s) by the sales figures to get the sum only for the sales that match your criteria.

For example, to sum the sales for "Widget A" in the "East" region, you could use:

```excel
=SUMPRODUCT((A2:A100="Widget A")*(B2:B100="East"), C2:C100)
```

This formula evaluates each row, checking whether it meets both conditions (product is "Widget A" and region is "East"), and then sums the corresponding sales figures from column C.

Dynamic Named Ranges for Flexible Formulas

Dynamic named ranges in Excel are named ranges that automatically adjust as data is added or removed. This feature is incredibly useful for analyses that need to accommodate growing datasets without manual range updates.

Creating a Dynamic Named Range:

Use the **OFFSET** function in conjunction with **COUNTA** (for non-numeric data) or **COUNT** (for numeric data) to create a dynamic range. The OFFSET function creates a reference shifted a certain number of rows and columns from a starting cell, with a specified height and width.

Example of Dynamic Named Range:
If you're tracking monthly sales in column A and expect to add new data regularly, you can create a dynamic named range that includes all existing sales data and expands automatically as new months are added.

To create a dynamic named range for sales data in column A starting from A2, you could use:
```excel
=OFFSET($A$2, 0, 0, COUNTA($A:$A)-1, 1)
```

This formula starts at A2 and expands downward to include all non-blank cells in column A. The "-1" in the formula accounts for excluding the header row from the count.

By leveraging **SUMPRODUCT** for advanced conditional sums and creating **dynamic named ranges**, you can significantly enhance the flexibility and efficiency of your Excel workbooks. These techniques allow for more sophisticated data analysis and ensure your formulas remain accurate as your data evolves. Practice incorporating these advanced strategies into your Excel projects to better manage and analyse complex datasets.

Dynamic Named Ranges for Flexible Formulas

Dynamic named ranges make your Excel workbooks more adaptable and your formulas more robust, especially as your data grows or changes over time. By automatically adjusting to include new data, dynamic named ranges ensure that your analyses, charts, and formulas always reflect the complete dataset without manual updates.

Implementing Dynamic Named Ranges

To fully harness the power of dynamic named ranges, you can use Excel's `OFFSET` function in combination with `COUNTA` for text data or `COUNT` for numerical data, as well as other functions like `MATCH` for even more flexibility.

Using OFFSET with COUNTA/COUNT:

The `OFFSET` function creates a range that starts at a specific point and extends for a specified number of rows and columns. When combined with `COUNTA` (which counts non-blank cells) or `COUNT` (which counts cells containing numbers), you create a range that automatically expands or contracts with your data.

Example for Numeric Data:
```excel
=OFFSET($A$1, 0, 0, COUNT($A:$A), 1)
```

This formula creates a dynamic range starting from cell A1, extending down as many rows as there are numbers in column A, and spanning one column wide.

Example for Text Data:
```excel
=OFFSET($A$1, 0, 0, COUNTA($A:$A), 1)
```

Similar to the numeric example, this range starts from A1 and includes as many rows as there are non-blank cells in column A, suitable for text data.

Expanding Beyond Single Columns:

While the examples above focus on a single column, you can adjust the `OFFSET` formula to cover multiple columns by changing the width parameter (the last number in the formula). For instance, to include the first three columns, change `1` to `3`.

Benefits and Uses of Dynamic Named Ranges

Automated Updates: As you add or remove data, dynamic named ranges adjust accordingly, ensuring that your formulas, PivotTables, and charts always use the entire dataset.

Simplified Formulas: Instead of updating range references in your formulas manually, you can use the name of your dynamic range, making formulas easier to read and maintain.

Enhanced Charts and PivotTables: Charts and PivotTables using dynamic named ranges automatically update to reflect new data, eliminating the need for manual adjustments.

Best Practices for Dynamic Named Ranges

Clearly Name Your Ranges: Choose names that clearly indicate the content or purpose of the range, such as "SalesData" or "CustomerList," to make your workbook easier to navigate.

Regularly Check Your Ranges: Especially in complex workbooks, ensure your dynamic ranges are correctly adjusting to your data. Adding a significant amount of data outside the expected type (e.g., text in a numerical column) might require adjustments to your setup.

Combine with Other Excel Features: Explore how dynamic named ranges can enhance other Excel functionalities, such as data validation lists, to make your entire workbook more dynamic and responsive to changes.

By incorporating dynamic named ranges into your Excel workbooks, you unlock a new level of flexibility and efficiency in your data analysis and reporting. This advanced technique is crucial for managing large datasets, ensuring your Excel projects remain accurate and up-to-date with minimal manual intervention. Practice setting up dynamic named ranges in your workbooks to become proficient in this valuable Excel feature.

Chapter 9

Introduction to Macros and VBA

Expanding your Excel skills to include macros and Visual Basic for Applications (VBA) can significantly increase your productivity by automating repetitive tasks and customising Excel to fit your specific needs. This chapter introduces you to the basics of recording macros for automating routine tasks and provides a brief introduction to VBA for more advanced automation possibilities.

Recording Basic Macros for Repetitive Tasks

Macros in Excel are a powerful feature that allows you to automate repetitive tasks. A macro records your actions in Excel and can replay them exactly, saving you time and effort.

How to Record a Macro:

1. **Prepare Your Data**: Before recording a macro, ensure your data is set up as you need it. The macro will record all your actions, so it's best to streamline your process first.

2. **Start Recording**: Go to the View tab, and in the Macros group, click on "Record Macro." A dialog box will appear where you can name your macro, assign a shortcut key (optional), and provide a description.

3. **Perform the Task**: Carry out the task you want to automate. This could be anything from formatting cells, applying filters, or entering formulas. Excel records all your actions.

4. **Stop Recording**: Once you have completed the task, go back to the View tab and click "Stop Recording." Your macro is now saved and can be run at any time to replicate the actions you recorded.

Running Your Macro:

- To run your macro, go to the View tab, click on "Macros," select "View Macros," choose the macro you want to run, and click "Run." Alternatively, if you assigned a shortcut key during the recording, you can use that key combination.

Tips for Effective Macro Recording:

Plan Your Actions: Before recording, plan the steps you need to take. Unnecessary actions will be recorded and replayed every time you run the macro.

Relative vs. Absolute References: By default, macros use absolute cell references. If you need your macro to work with cells relative to the currently selected cell, choose "Use Relative References" before you start recording.

Test Your Macro: After recording, test your macro on different data sets to ensure it works as expected.

Brief Introduction to VBA for Automation

While recording macros is straightforward and powerful for many tasks, some automations require more flexibility and control than what macro recording offers. This is where VBA comes into play.

What is VBA?

- VBA, or Visual Basic for Applications, is a programming language provided by Excel that allows you to create more complex macros. With VBA, you can automate almost any action you can perform in Excel, including manipulating data, formatting cells, and even interacting with other applications.

Accessing the VBA Editor:

- You can access the VBA Editor by pressing `Alt + F11` in Excel. This opens the editor where you can write, edit, and manage your VBA code.

Writing a Simple VBA Macro:

1. **Insert a Module**: In the VBA Editor, right-click on any of the objects in the Project Explorer window, choose "Insert," and then "Module." This creates a new module where you can write your code.

2. **Write Your Macro**: In the module, you can write your VBA code. For example, a simple macro to display a message box could look like this:

```vba
Sub ShowMessage()
    MsgBox "Hello, Excel World!"
```

```
End Sub
```

This macro, when run, will display a message box with the text "Hello, Excel World!"

3. **Run Your Macro**: You can run your VBA macro directly from the VBA Editor by pressing `F5` or by using the "Run" button.

Learning VBA:

- Learning VBA opens up a new world of possibilities in Excel. Start with simple tasks and gradually tackle more complex problems. There are numerous resources available online, including tutorials, forums, and courses, to help you on your journey.

By incorporating macros and VBA into your Excel toolkit, you can automate a wide range of tasks, from the simple and repetitive to the complex and customised. This not only saves time but also allows you to utilise Excel's full potential, making your workflows more efficient and your data analysis more powerful.

Brief Introduction to VBA for Automation

Visual Basic for Applications (VBA) is a powerful scripting language built into Microsoft Excel that allows users to automate almost any aspect of the application. From simple tasks like formatting cells to complex data analysis and interfacing with other Office applications, VBA extends the functionality of Excel far beyond its standard capabilities. This introduction will guide you through the basics of using VBA for automation, providing the foundation you need to begin exploring the vast potential of Excel macros.

Understanding VBA

What is VBA?

- VBA stands for Visual Basic for Applications, a programming language provided by Microsoft Office programs. It enables the automation of tasks within Excel, allowing you to create custom functions, automate repetitive tasks, and develop complex macros that can perform operations with the click of a button.

Why Use VBA?

- Automation: Automate repetitive Excel tasks, saving time and reducing errors.
- Customisation: Tailor Excel to meet your specific needs, creating custom solutions that standard Excel functions can't achieve.
- Integration: Interact with other Microsoft Office applications, such as Word and Outlook, allowing for seamless data exchange and workflow automation across applications.

Getting Started with VBA

Accessing the VBA Editor:

- You can open the VBA Editor by pressing `Alt + F11` in Excel. This environment is where you will write, edit, and debug your VBA code. The editor consists of a Project Explorer, a Code Window, and various other tools to help you manage your VBA projects.

Writing Your First Macro:

- A macro in VBA is simply a procedure that performs actions in Excel. To create a macro, you need to write a Sub procedure. Here's an example of a simple macro that inserts the text "Hello, World!" into cell A1 of the active worksheet:

```vba
Sub HelloWorld()
    Range("A1").Value = "Hello, World!"
End Sub
```

- To run this macro, you can press `F5` while in the VBA Editor with the cursor inside the procedure code.

Understanding VBA Syntax:

- VBA syntax defines how you write statements in VBA. It includes the use of keywords, variables, loops, conditional statements, and more. Mastering VBA syntax is essential for writing effective and efficient macros.

Automating Tasks with VBA

Looping and Conditionals:

- VBA allows you to use loops (e.g., `For`, `While`) to repeat actions and conditional statements (e.g., `If`) to make decisions within your macros. This is particularly useful for processing collections of data in Excel sheets.

Interacting with Excel Objects:

- Excel VBA operates on objects (e.g., Workbook, Worksheet, Range). Learning to manipulate these objects is key to automating tasks in Excel. For example, you can automate the process of formatting cells, creating charts, or filtering data by interacting with the appropriate objects.

Error Handling:

- To make your macros more robust, VBA provides error-handling capabilities. Using the `On Error` statement, you can define what happens when an error occurs, ensuring your macro can gracefully handle unexpected situations.

Advancing Your VBA Skills

As you become more comfortable with the basics of VBA, you can explore more advanced topics, including creating user forms for data entry, accessing external databases, and optimising your VBA code for performance.

Resources for Learning VBA:

- There are countless resources available to help you learn VBA, from online tutorials and forums to comprehensive guidebooks. Taking advantage of these resources can accelerate your learning and enable you to leverage the full power of Excel VBA.

Starting with VBA might seem daunting, but by breaking down tasks into manageable pieces and practising regularly, you'll quickly gain confidence. Remember, the goal of using VBA is to make your work in Excel more efficient and effective, opening up new possibilities for data analysis and task automation.

Chapter 10

Charts and Graphs

Charts and graphs are essential tools in Excel that allow you to visually represent data, making it easier to understand trends, patterns, and outliers. Excel offers a wide variety of chart types, including bar, line, pie, and more, each suited to different kinds of data and analysis. This chapter guides you through creating and customising these charts, as well as exploring advanced charting techniques like combo charts and using a secondary axis.

Creating and Customising Charts: Bar, Line, Pie, and More

Creating Charts in Excel:

1. **Select Your Data**: Before creating a chart, select the data range that you want to visualise. Include any row or column labels if they should be part of the chart.

2. **Choose the Chart Type**: Navigate to the Insert tab on the Ribbon. Here, you'll find a variety of chart types to choose from, including Bar, Line, Pie, and others. Click on the one that best suits your data.

3. **Insert the Chart**: After selecting a chart type, Excel will automatically generate the chart and place it in your worksheet. You can then move and resize the chart as needed.

Customising Charts:

Excel offers numerous customisation options to help you tailor your charts to your specific needs.

Chart Elements: Add, remove, or modify chart elements like titles, legends, and labels through the Chart Elements button (a plus sign) next to the chart.

Chart Styles: Change the overall look of your chart using the Chart Styles options. You can choose from a variety of predefined styles and colour schemes.

Data Series: Adjust individual data series within the chart, such as changing the colour or type of bars in a bar chart. Right-click on the series to see formatting options.

Axes: Customise the chart axes to improve readability. This might include changing the scale of the axes, adjusting the interval of tick marks, or formatting the text.

Advanced Chart Techniques: Combo Charts, Secondary Axis

Combo Charts:

When you want to visualise two different types of data together, a combo chart can be very effective. Combo charts combine two or more chart types, such as a line chart and a bar chart, to provide a clearer view of complex data.

Creating a Combo Chart: Select your data, then go to the Insert tab and click on the "Combo Chart" dropdown in the Charts group. Choose one of the predefined combinations or select "Create Custom Combo Chart" to customise further.

Using a Secondary Axis:

In some cases, you might want to compare two data series that have different scales. Using a secondary axis allows you to plot data on two different scales in the same chart.

Adding a Secondary Axis: After creating your chart, click on the data series you want to plot on the secondary axis. Go to the Format Data Series pane, and check the option for "Secondary Axis." This will add a new vertical axis to the right side of your chart, allowing you to adjust its scale independently.

Chart Design Tips:

Keep It Simple: Avoid adding too many elements to your chart, as this can make it cluttered and difficult to read. Focus on the data you want to highlight.

Label Clearly: Make sure all parts of your chart are clearly labelled, including axes and data series, so that viewers can easily understand what they are looking at.

Use Colours Wisely: Use colour to enhance readability and highlight key data points, but be mindful of colorblind viewers and ensure there is sufficient contrast.

Creating and customising charts in Excel allows you to present your data in a visually appealing and easily digestible format. By mastering both basic and advanced charting techniques, you can enhance your data analysis and reporting, making it more impactful and accessible to your audience.

Advanced Chart Techniques: Combo Charts, Secondary Axis

When working with diverse data sets or aiming to highlight different types of information within a single visualisation, Excel's advanced charting techniques, such as combo charts and the use of a secondary axis, become invaluable. These techniques allow for a more nuanced analysis and presentation of data, catering to complex comparisons and data relationships.

Combo Charts

What Are Combo Charts?

Combo charts combine two or more chart types (e.g., column and line chart) into a single visualisation, making it easier to compare different data sets or highlight relationships between them.

They are particularly useful when your data includes both cumulative totals and individual components or when you want to show two different types of information, such as quantities and percentages.

Creating a Combo Chart:

1. **Select Your Data**: Start by selecting the data you want to visualise. This includes any categories and the different data series you plan to compare.

2. **Insert a Combo Chart**: Navigate to the Insert tab, click the Combo Chart dropdown in the Charts group, and select "Create Custom Combo Chart." Excel will display the "Insert Chart" dialog.

3. **Customise Chart Types**: In the "Insert Chart" dialog, you can assign different chart types to each data series. For example, you might choose a column chart for sales data and a line chart for the percentage growth. Ensure to check the box for "Secondary Axis" for the series that will use it.

4. **Refine and Finalise**: Once you've assigned chart types and axes, click OK to insert your combo chart. You can then further customise the chart using the Chart Tools on the Ribbon, adjusting elements like the chart title, axis titles, and data labels for clarity.

Using a Secondary Axis

When to Use a Secondary Axis:

A secondary axis is useful when comparing two data series that have different scales or units of measurement. By plotting one series on the primary axis and the other on the secondary axis, you can create a clearer, more effective comparison.

Adding a Secondary Axis:

1. **Create Your Chart**: After inserting a basic chart that includes the two data series you wish to compare, select the chart to activate the Chart Tools on the Ribbon.

2. **Assign a Secondary Axis**: Click on the series that you want to move to the secondary axis to select it. Then, under the Chart Tools Format tab, click "Format Selection." In the Format Data Series pane, choose "Secondary Axis." This action will add a new vertical axis to the right side of your chart.

3. **Customise Your Axes**: You can customise both the primary and secondary axes independently. This includes adjusting the scale, changing the axis titles, and formatting the text. Proper customization

ensures both data series are presented clearly and accurately.

Tips for Effective Combo Charts and Secondary Axes

Choose Compatible Chart Types: When creating combo charts, select chart types that complement each other and make the data comparison intuitive, such as bars for one series and lines for another.

Balance Your Axes: Ensure the scales on your primary and secondary axes are set in a way that makes the comparison meaningful. Avoid scales that could mislead or confuse the viewer.

Highlight Key Data Points: Use data labels or markers to highlight important values or trends in your chart. This can draw attention to significant insights or changes in the data.

Maintain Clarity: While combo charts and secondary axes can provide depth to your analysis, clarity should always be a priority. Ensure your chart remains readable and understandable, avoiding overcrowding with too many data series or overly complex configurations.

By mastering advanced chart techniques like combo charts and the use of a secondary axis, you can elevate your data visualisation skills in Excel. These techniques allow for a more sophisticated analysis and presentation of data, enabling you to convey complex insights in a clear and impactful manner.

Chapter 11

Conditional Formatting

Conditional formatting in Excel is a powerful feature that allows you to dynamically apply formatting to cells based on the data they contain. This means you can automatically change the appearance of cells, rows, or columns based on specific criteria, such as values being above or below a certain threshold, duplicates, or even based on the value of another cell. This chapter explores how to use conditional formatting to highlight data dynamically, and introduces advanced formatting options like data bars, colour scales, and icon sets.

Highlighting Data Dynamically

What Is Dynamic Highlighting?

Dynamic highlighting uses conditional formatting to visually emphasise or de-emphasize cells in your data based on their values or conditions. This can help users quickly identify trends, outliers, or important data points within a large dataset.

Applying Conditional Formatting:

1. **Select Your Data**: Start by selecting the cells or range where you want to apply conditional formatting.

2. **Access Conditional Formatting Options**: Navigate to the Home tab on the Ribbon, and in the Styles group, click on "Conditional Formatting." You'll see a dropdown menu with various options.

3. **Choose a Rule**: Select from predefined rules like "Highlight Cell Rules" or "Top/Bottom Rules" for common conditions, or choose "New Rule" for more customised conditions. For example, you can set a rule to highlight all cells that are greater than a certain value.

4. **Customise the Format**: After choosing or defining a rule, specify the formatting options, such as changing the cell's background colour, text colour, or applying a specific font style.

5. **Apply and Review**: Once you apply the formatting, Excel will automatically update the appearance of the cells based on the criteria you set. If data changes, the formatting updates in real-time to reflect the new values.

Advanced Formatting Options

Data Bars:

Data bars are a form of conditional formatting that adds a coloured bar inside a cell, with the length of the bar representing the value in the cell relative to the other selected cells.

Applying Data Bars: Select your data range, go to Conditional Formatting > Data Bars, and choose from the gradient or solid fill options. Customise the colour to fit your presentation needs.

Colour Scales:

Colour scales change the background colour of each cell in a range based on its value. The colour transition can represent a gradient from low to high, making it easy to visualise the distribution of values.

Using Color Scales: After selecting your data, click Conditional Formatting > Color Scales and select a predefined colour scale or customise your own. Each colour scale provides a visual heat map of your data.

Icon Sets:

Icon sets add icons to your cells, such as arrows or traffic lights, based on their value. This is useful for categorising data into different tiers or statuses at a glance.

Implementing Icon Sets: Choose your range, then select Conditional Formatting > Icon Sets. Pick an icon set that suits your data's narrative. You can customise which icons appear for specific value ranges or thresholds.

Tips for Using Conditional Formatting

Clear Rules: Regularly review and clear unnecessary rules to prevent conflicts and ensure your workbook performs optimally. Conditional Formatting > Clear Rules lets you remove formatting from selected cells or the entire sheet.

Manage Rules: Use the Conditional Formatting > Manage Rules dialog to edit, delete, or change the priority of your formatting rules. This is especially helpful in complex worksheets with multiple conditions.

Efficient Use: While conditional formatting is powerful, using it excessively or on very large data sets can slow down your workbook. Apply it judiciously to maintain performance.

Conditional formatting is an effective tool for making your Excel workbooks more intuitive and visually appealing. By highlighting data dynamically, you can draw attention to key insights and make your data much easier to analyse at a glance. Whether you're using simple colour highlights, data bars, colour scales, or icon sets, conditional formatting can transform how you present and interpret your data in Excel.

Data Bars, Color Scales, and Icon Sets

After establishing the basics of conditional formatting and its capability to dynamically highlight data, let's dive deeper into the more advanced features: data bars, colour scales, and icon sets. These features provide a visually intuitive way to analyse and compare your data directly within the cells of your Excel worksheets.

Data Bars

What Are Data Bars?

Data bars add a visual bar within your cells, with the length of the bar representing the cell's value in proportion to other selected cells. This makes it easy to visually compare the magnitude of values across a range.

Applying Data Bars:

1. **Select the Range**: Highlight the cells you want to format with data bars.
2. **Choose Data Bars**: Go to the Home tab, click on "Conditional Formatting," hover over "Data Bars," and choose from the available gradient or solid fill styles.
3. **Customisation Options**: For more control, after clicking on "Data Bars," select "More Rules." Here, you can adjust settings like the bar colour, whether to show the bar only, and how to scale the bars against other values in the selection.

Colour Scales

What Are Color Scales?

Colour scales change the background colour of cells within a range based on their values. They provide a heat map effect, allowing you to quickly spot high and low values through colour gradients.

Using Color Scales:

1. **Select Your Data**: Choose the cells you wish to format.
2. **Apply Color Scales**: Navigate to "Conditional Formatting" on the Home tab, select "Color Scales," and pick a predefined colour scale. Each scale offers a different way to visualise the data, from green-yellow-red gradients to more nuanced colour transitions.
3. **Customisation**: For a more tailored approach, select "More Rules" from the Color Scales menu to define your own colour gradients and set the minimum, midpoint, and maximum conditions based on your data's specifics.

Icon Sets

What Are Icon Sets?

Icon sets allow you to categorise data in a range by adding icons next to your values, such as directional arrows, traffic lights, or ratings. This method is excellent for quick visual assessments of performance or status.

Implementing Icon Sets:

1. **Highlight the Target Cells**: Choose the range where you want icons to appear.
2. **Select an Icon Set**: Click on "Conditional Formatting," move to "Icon Sets," and choose one that fits your data presentation needs. Excel offers a variety of icons that can suit different data types and comparisons.
3. **Adjusting Criteria**: By default, Excel divides your data into thirds for most icon sets. To customise this, go to "Manage Rules" under the Conditional Formatting options, where you can set specific thresholds for when each icon should be used. This is particularly useful for data that does not naturally divide into equal parts or for emphasising specific ranges.

Tips for Advanced Conditional Formatting

Balance Visuals with Readability: While these advanced conditional formatting options can significantly enhance data visualisation, it's important to ensure that your sheet remains readable and not overwhelmed by colours or icons.

Use for Comparative Analysis: Data bars, colour scales, and icon sets are most effective when used to compare and contrast data within the same dataset. They help highlight trends, outliers, or specific ranges that might require attention.

Combine with Other Excel Features: Advanced conditional formatting works well in conjunction with Excel's other analytical tools, like PivotTables and filters, to provide deep insights into your data.

Advanced conditional formatting techniques such as data bars, colour scales, and icon sets provide powerful ways to visually interpret and present data in Excel. By customising these features to suit your data, you can create dynamic, informative, and visually appealing spreadsheets that make data analysis more intuitive and accessible.

Chapter 12

Conditional Formatting

Conditional formatting in Excel is a dynamic tool that adjusts the formatting of cells within your spreadsheet based on the data they contain. This feature can significantly enhance your data's readability by visually emphasising key information through colour coding, icons, or data bars. This chapter delves into how to utilise conditional formatting to highlight data dynamically, and introduces the use of data bars, colour scales, and icon sets for advanced data visualisation.

Highlighting Data Dynamically

Dynamic Highlighting with Conditional Formatting:

Conditional formatting enables you to automatically apply specific formatting to cells that meet certain criteria. This dynamic highlighting can help users quickly identify trends, anomalies, or specific conditions within their data.

Skipton Tech

Steps to Apply Conditional Formatting:

1. **Select the Data Range**: Begin by selecting the cells you wish to format. You can highlight individual cells, ranges, or entire rows/columns.

2. **Access Conditional Formatting**: Navigate to the Home tab on the Ribbon. In the Styles group, click on "Conditional Formatting" to display the dropdown menu with various formatting options.

3. **Choose a Formatting Rule**: Excel offers several preset rules for common conditions such as greater than, less than, equal to, between, or specific text occurrences. Select the rule that matches your criteria.

4. **Customise the Formatting**: After selecting a rule, you'll be prompted to define the specific criteria and choose the formatting style. You can select from predefined formats or create your own by specifying font colour, cell colour, and other formatting details.

5. **Apply and Review**: Once applied, Excel automatically formats the cells based on your criteria. If data changes, the formatting updates accordingly to reflect the new values.

Advanced Visualisation with Data Bars, Color Scales, and Icon Sets

Data Bars:

Data bars add a visual element within the cell, with the bar's length representing the cell's value relative to other selected cells. This makes comparative analysis visually intuitive.

Applying Data Bars: After selecting your data range, click "Conditional Formatting" > "Data Bars" and choose from the gradient or solid fill options. Excel offers a range of colours to enhance your data presentation visually.

Colour Scales:

Colour scales apply a colour gradient across your selected cells, with the gradient reflecting the cell's value. This creates a heat map effect, allowing for quick identification of high and low values.

Using Colour Scales: Select your data, then choose "Conditional Formatting" > "Colour Scales." Excel provides a variety of predefined colour gradients. Select one to automatically apply a visual heatmap to your data.

Icon Sets:

Icon sets categorise and prioritise data by adding specific icons next to your values. This is effective for quickly conveying information such as performance ratings, priority levels, or directional trends.

Implementing Icon Sets: Highlight your desired range and click "Conditional Formatting" > "Icon Sets." Choose an icon set that matches your data interpretation needs. Excel will automatically assign icons based on the value distribution in your selected range.

Tips for Using Conditional Formatting Effectively

Use Sparingly: While conditional formatting can significantly enhance your spreadsheet's usability, using too many different formats simultaneously can lead to visual clutter and confusion. Aim for simplicity and clarity.

Consistency is Key: Use consistent formatting rules and styles throughout your workbook to ensure that your visual cues are easily understood.

Review and Adjust: Periodically review your conditional formatting rules to ensure they remain relevant as your data changes or your analysis evolves. Excel allows you to manage and edit existing rules through the "Manage Rules" option in the conditional formatting menu.

Conditional formatting is a versatile tool in Excel that, when used effectively, can transform how you present and interpret data. By dynamically highlighting key information and employing advanced visualisation techniques like data bars, colour scales, and icon sets, you can create more informative, engaging, and accessible spreadsheets.

Managing and Editing Conditional Formatting Rules

After applying conditional formatting to highlight data dynamically and utilising advanced visualisation techniques like data bars, colour scales, and icon sets, it's crucial to understand how to manage and edit these rules. Efficient management ensures that your conditional formatting remains accurate and relevant as your data changes or as your analysis evolves.

Reviewing Existing Conditional Formatting Rules

Excel allows you to view and edit all the conditional formatting rules applied to a worksheet, providing a comprehensive overview that helps in managing complex formatting scenarios.

Steps to Review Conditional Formatting Rules:

1. **Accessing the Rules Manager**: To view all conditional formatting rules in the current worksheet, go to the Home tab, click on "Conditional Formatting," and select "Manage Rules." The Conditional Formatting Rules Manager dialog box will appear, listing all the rules for the selected worksheet or workbook.

2. **Understanding the Rules Manager**: In the Rules Manager, you can see the specifics of each rule, including the range it applies to, the formatting criteria, and the format itself. Rules are listed in the order they are applied, which is important because Excel stops evaluating rules once a condition is met, unless the "Stop If True" check box is cleared.

Editing Conditional Formatting Rules

Over time, you may need to adjust your conditional formatting rules to better fit your evolving data or analysis needs. The Rules Manager provides a central location to make these adjustments.

How to Edit a Rule:

1. **Select the Rule**: In the Conditional Formatting Rules Manager, click on the rule you wish to edit. This will enable the "Edit Rule" button.

2. **Modify the Rule**: Click "Edit Rule" to open the Edit Formatting Rule dialog box. Here, you can change the rule type, the formatting criteria, and the format. For example, you might adjust the threshold for a "greater than" rule or choose a different colour for highlighting.

3. **Applying Changes**: After making your adjustments, click "OK" to close the Edit Rule dialog, and then "OK" again in the Rules Manager to apply your changes. The conditional formatting in your worksheet will update to reflect the edited rule.

Deleting Conditional Formatting Rules

If a conditional formatting rule is no longer needed or if you're simplifying your worksheet's formatting, you can delete individual rules through the Rules Manager.

1. **Open the Rules Manager**: Navigate to "Conditional Formatting" > "Manage Rules."

2. **Select the Rule to Delete**: In the Rules Manager, click on the rule you want to remove.

3. **Delete the Rule**: With the rule selected, click the "Delete Rule" button. Confirm the deletion if prompted. The rule will be removed, and the conditional formatting it applied will no longer affect the selected cells.

Tips for Effective Conditional Formatting Rule Management

Prioritise Your Rules: Remember that rules are applied in the order they are listed. You can use the "Move Up" and "Move Down" buttons in the Rules Manager to change the order and control which rules take precedence.

Use Clear and Descriptive Names: When creating or editing rules, use names that clearly describe the rule's purpose. This practice makes it easier to identify and manage rules, especially in workbooks with multiple conditional formatting applications.

Regularly Audit Your Rules: Periodically review your conditional formatting rules to ensure they're still relevant and correctly applied. This is especially important for workbooks that undergo frequent updates or are used by multiple people.

By effectively managing and editing your conditional formatting rules, you can ensure that your Excel workbooks remain visually informative and analytically precise. Regular review and adjustment of these rules allow your data visualisations to evolve in line with your data analysis needs, maintaining clarity and enhancing insight.

Chapter 13

Dashboards and Reporting

In today's data-driven environment, dashboards and reports serve as critical tools for summarising, visualising, and communicating key information. Effective dashboards transform complex datasets into accessible insights, enabling decision-makers to grasp trends, metrics, and anomalies at a glance. This section focuses on the foundational principles of effective dashboard design, guiding you through creating impactful and user-friendly dashboards in Excel.

Principles of Effective Dashboards

Clarity and Purpose:

Define the Dashboard's Objective: Before starting, clearly define what the dashboard is intended to achieve. Understanding its purpose, whether for tracking performance, analysing trends, or supporting decisions, will guide your design choices.
Simplify the Presentation: Avoid clutter by only including elements that contribute to the

dashboard's objectives. Use whitespace effectively to separate different sections and ensure the dashboard isn't overwhelming.

Audience-Centric Design:

Know Your Audience: Tailor the complexity, terminology, and data presented to match the knowledge and needs of your intended audience. What's intuitive to a data analyst might not be for someone from a different background.
Accessibility: Design your dashboard to be accessible to all users, including those with disabilities. Use contrasting colours for text and background and ensure charts are understandable even in black and white.

Data Visualisation Choices:

Select Appropriate Chart Types: Choose chart types that best represent the data and make comparisons easy. For instance, use bar charts for comparing categories, line charts for trends over time, and pie charts for showing proportions.
Consistent Use of Colours: Apply colour consistently across your dashboard to represent similar data points or categories, enhancing readability. Reserve bright or distinct colours for highlighting critical data or exceptions.

Interactivity and Flexibility:

Incorporate Interactive Elements: Where applicable, use slicers, dropdowns, or form controls to allow users to interact with the dashboard. This enables them to explore the data in ways that are meaningful to them.

Adaptability: Design your dashboard to easily accommodate updates or changes in data. Use dynamic ranges and formulas that automatically adjust as new data is added.

Accuracy and Timeliness:

Ensure Data Integrity: Verify that the data underlying your dashboard is accurate and up-to-date. Inaccurate data can lead to wrong conclusions and undermine trust in the dashboard.

Refresh Data Regularly: Automate data refreshes if possible, or provide clear instructions for manually updating the dashboard to ensure it remains relevant.

Performance Optimisation:

Optimise for Performance: Large datasets and complex calculations can slow down your dashboard. Optimise data queries and calculations, and consider using PivotTables and aggregated data to improve performance.

Implementing Dashboard Principles in Excel

When implementing these principles in Excel, leverage the software's robust features to create dynamic and interactive dashboards:

- Use **PivotTables** and **PivotCharts** for summarising and visualising data dynamically.
- Apply **conditional formatting** to automatically highlight key metrics or trends.
- Incorporate **charts** and **graphs** that align with your data's narrative and your audience's expectations.
- Utilise **form controls** and **ActiveX controls** for creating interactive elements that allow users to customise their view of the data.

By adhering to these principles, you can create Excel dashboards that not only convey critical insights but also engage and inform your audience effectively. Remember, the best dashboards are those that turn data into actionable intelligence, enabling users to derive meaningful conclusions quickly and efficiently.

Integrating charts, PivotTables, and Conditional Formatting

Integrating charts, PivotTables, and conditional formatting into your Excel dashboards and reports is essential for creating dynamic, informative, and visually appealing presentations of your data. This integration allows you to represent complex information succinctly, highlight key insights, and enable interactive data exploration. Here's how to effectively combine these powerful Excel features to enhance your dashboards and reports.

Integrating Charts

Choosing the Right Chart Types:

Understand Your Data: Select chart types that best fit the nature of your data and the story you want to tell. For example, use line charts for trends over time, bar or column charts for comparisons among items, and pie charts for showing proportions within a dataset.

Customise for Clarity: Tailor your charts to enhance readability—adjust colours, add labels, and fine-tune axes. Keep the design simple and focused on conveying the intended message.

Use Tables for Source Data: Convert your data range into a Table (Insert > Table). Charts based on Table data automatically update when new data is added to the Table, keeping your charts current without manual adjustments.

Leveraging PivotTables

Summarising Data:

Create PivotTables for Dynamic Summaries: PivotTables are ideal for aggregating and summarising large datasets. They allow you to quickly slice and dice your data, providing insights into patterns and trends.

Integrating with Charts – PivotCharts:

Visualise PivotTable Data: Use PivotCharts to turn PivotTable analyses into visual representations. PivotCharts maintain a link to their PivotTable, enabling dynamic updates and interactive exploration of the data.

Slicers for Interactivity:

Add Slicers for Easy Filtering: Slicers provide a user-friendly way to filter data in PivotTables and

PivotCharts. They offer a visual interface that lets users quickly segment and refine the data displayed in your dashboard.

Applying Conditional Formatting

Highlighting Key Data:

Use Conditional Formatting to Draw Attention: Apply conditional formatting to dynamically highlight important values, trends, or variations in your data. Use colour scales, data bars, or icon sets to visually annotate data points based on specific criteria.

Interactive Data Exploration:

Enhance Table Interactivity: Apply conditional formatting within Excel Tables to enable dynamic visual exploration of the data. As users sort and filter the Table, the conditional formatting adjusts to highlight relevant patterns and insights.

Best Practices for Integration

Maintain a Clean Layout:

Organise Thoughtfully: Position your charts, PivotTables, and key metrics strategically within your dashboard. Ensure that the layout is intuitive and guides the viewer through the data story logically and effectively.

Ensure Consistency:

Use a Unified Design Language: Apply consistent styling across your charts, tables, and conditional formatting to create a cohesive look and feel. This includes using a harmonised colour scheme, fonts, and design elements.

Optimise for Performance:

Balance Detail and Performance: Complex calculations, numerous PivotTables, and extensive conditional formatting can impact dashboard performance. Regularly review and optimise your dashboard elements to ensure smooth operation, especially when dealing with large datasets.

Integrating charts, PivotTables, and conditional formatting in Excel allows you to build comprehensive, interactive, and visually engaging dashboards and reports. By following these guidelines and best practices, you can transform raw data into meaningful insights, enabling informed decision-making and effective communication of your analysis.

Interactive controls (Form Controls, ActiveX)

Interactive controls, such as Form Controls and ActiveX Controls, play a crucial role in enhancing the interactivity and user engagement of Excel dashboards and reports. These controls allow users to interact with the dashboard in real-time, filtering data, adjusting parameters, and customising views according to their specific needs. This section explores how to incorporate these interactive elements into your dashboards and reports for a dynamic data exploration experience.

Form Controls

Introduction to Form Controls:

Form Controls are simple interactive elements designed for user interaction within Excel sheets. They include buttons, check boxes, combo boxes, list boxes, spin buttons, option buttons, and scroll bars. Form Controls are straightforward to use and are compatible with most Excel versions, making them ideal for adding interactivity to dashboards.

Using Form Controls in Dashboards:

Buttons: Create a button to refresh data or execute a specific macro.

Check Boxes: Use check boxes for users to toggle data series or categories on and off within charts or tables.

Combo Boxes and List Boxes: Implement combo boxes or list boxes for users to select from a range of options, dynamically filtering data displayed in PivotTables, charts, or conditional formatting areas.

Spin Buttons and Scroll Bars: Add spin buttons or scroll bars to allow users to scroll through date ranges, financial scenarios, or other incrementally changing data, updating dashboard elements in real-time.

Implementing Form Controls:

1. **Inserting a Control**: Go to the Developer tab on the Ribbon, click "Insert," and choose the desired Form Control.

2. **Configuring the Control**: After placing the control on your dashboard, right-click it to access properties or link it to a specific cell or macro. This

linkage dictates the control's behaviour and its impact on the dashboard's data or visuals.

3. **Designing for Usability**: Position controls strategically within your dashboard, ensuring they are accessible and clearly labelled for easy use.

ActiveX Controls

Introduction to ActiveX Controls:

ActiveX Controls offer a more sophisticated level of interactivity and customization compared to Form Controls. With features like rich formatting options and the ability to contain complex scripts, ActiveX Controls are powerful tools for creating highly interactive and responsive dashboards. However, they are only supported on Windows versions of Excel.

Incorporating ActiveX Controls:

Richer User Interaction: Use ActiveX Controls for complex interactions, such as text input fields for dynamic queries or sliders with customised increments.

Event-Driven Programming: ActiveX Controls can trigger VBA scripts or macros in response to user actions (e.g., clicking a button or changing a text box), allowing for real-time data processing and dashboard updates.

Implementing ActiveX Controls:

1. **Adding an ActiveX Control**: On the Developer tab, click "Insert" and select an ActiveX Control. Draw it on your dashboard where you want the control to appear.
2. **Configuring and Customising**: Right-click the control to access its properties, where you can customise its appearance, set its properties, and write event-handling VBA code for actions like clicks or value changes.
3. **Security Considerations**: Because ActiveX Controls can run VBA code, ensure your dashboard and its source are trusted, especially when sharing with others.

Best Practices for Using Interactive Controls

Clarity and Purpose: Ensure each interactive control has a clear purpose and is intuitively understandable by the dashboard users. Tooltips or brief instructions can enhance usability.
Testing Across Environments: Especially important for dashboards that will be shared widely, test your interactive controls across different

versions of Excel and operating systems to ensure compatibility and functionality.

Balancing Functionality and Performance: Interactive controls, particularly ActiveX Controls with complex scripts, can impact dashboard performance. Regularly review and optimise to maintain responsiveness.

Integrating interactive controls into Excel dashboards transforms static reports into dynamic tools for analysis and decision-making. By carefully selecting and implementing Form Controls and ActiveX Controls, you can create engaging, user-friendly dashboards that empower users to explore data in meaningful ways.

Chapter 14

Efficiency Boosters

In Excel, efficiency isn't just about what you do; it's also about how quickly and smoothly you can do it. Keyboard shortcuts are invaluable tools for speeding up navigation, formatting, and formula entry, allowing you to perform tasks without taking your hands off the keyboard to reach for the mouse. This chapter covers essential keyboard shortcuts that can significantly enhance your productivity in Excel.

Keyboard Shortcuts for Navigation

Navigating through your workbook efficiently is crucial for productivity, especially when working with large datasets or multiple worksheets.

Move Between Cells:

Arrow Keys: Navigate to adjacent cells.
Ctrl + Arrow Key: Jump to the edge of data regions.
Home: Move to the beginning of a row.

Ctrl + Home: Jump to the first cell of a worksheet (A1).

Sheet Navigation:

Ctrl + Page Up/Page Down: Move between sheets in a workbook.

Navigating Within a Cell:

F2: Edit the active cell, placing the cursor at the end of the cell content.
Home/End (While Editing): Move to the beginning or end of the cell content.

Keyboard Shortcuts for Formatting

Applying formatting quickly can make data more readable and your worksheets more professional-looking without disrupting your workflow.

Apply Basic Formats:

Ctrl + B: Bold the selected text or cell.
Ctrl + I: Italicise the selected text or cell.
Ctrl + U: Underline the selected text or cell.

Adjust Cell Formats:

Ctrl + Shift + $: Apply currency format.
Ctrl + Shift + %: Apply percentage format.
Ctrl + Shift + ~: Apply the general number format.
Ctrl + Shift + ^: Apply scientific notation format.
Ctrl + Shift + #: Apply date format.

Adjust Column Width and Row Height:

Alt + H, O, I: AutoFit column width.
Alt + H, O, A: AutoFit row height.

Keyboard Shortcuts for Formulas

Entering formulas is a fundamental part of working with Excel. Speeding up this process can save considerable time.

Entering and Editing Formulas:

F2: Edit the selected cell.
Ctrl + Shift + Enter: Enter an array formula (for versions prior to dynamic arrays in Excel).
Alt + =: Automatically sum the selected cells above or to the left of the active cell.

Function Insertion:

Shift + F3: Open the Insert Function dialog box to search for and insert functions.

Formula Auditing:

F4 (After Typing a Cell Reference): Cycle through absolute and relative references.

Alt + M, V: Evaluate the formula step-by-step (Formula Auditing > Evaluate Formula).

General Productivity Boosters

Quick Access to Ribbon Commands:

Alt: Activate the Ribbon's keyboard shortcuts. Pressing Alt reveals letters for each tab on the Ribbon. Continue pressing the corresponding letters to navigate and activate specific commands.

Creating a New Worksheet:

Shift + F11: Insert a new worksheet into the workbook.

Saving Your Workbook:

Ctrl + S: Save the workbook.

Understanding and utilising these keyboard shortcuts in Excel can dramatically increase your efficiency, allowing you to perform a wide array of tasks rapidly and with ease. As you become more familiar with these shortcuts, you'll find your workflow becoming smoother and your productivity soaring.

Tips for Faster Data Entry

Beyond mastering keyboard shortcuts, there are numerous strategies and tips you can employ to speed up data entry and editing in Excel. Efficient data management not only saves time but also minimises errors, ensuring your datasets are accurate and up-to-date. This section provides practical advice for enhancing your data entry and editing processes in Excel.

Utilise Excel Tables:

- Convert your data range into an Excel Table (Insert > Table). Tables offer several benefits for data entry, including automatic expansion to include new data, column headers that remain visible at the top of the screen as you scroll, and the ability to quickly add new rows that automatically match the formatting of the rows above.

AutoFill for Repetitive Data:

- Use the AutoFill feature to quickly populate cells. Type the beginning of a pattern (e.g., days of the week, months, sequential numbers), select the cells, then drag the fill handle (a small square at the bottom right corner of the selection) down or across to complete the series.

Flash Fill for Pattern Recognition:

- Flash Fill (Data > Flash Fill or Ctrl + E) is a powerful tool that recognizes patterns in your data entry and automatically fills other cells accordingly. For example, if you're separating first and last names into two columns, once you've manually completed a few entries, Flash Fill can automatically complete the rest.

Data Validation for Consistency:

- Implement Data Validation (Data > Data Validation) to restrict the type of data or the values that users can enter into a cell. This is useful for maintaining data integrity and ensuring consistency, especially when multiple users are entering data.

Tips for Efficient Data Editing

Find and Replace for Quick Edits:

- Use Find and Replace (Ctrl + H) to quickly make bulk changes to your data, such as correcting a recurring typo, updating a product name, or changing a date format across the entire dataset.

Use Formulas for Mass Updates:

- Instead of manually updating each cell, use formulas to make changes in bulk. For instance, if you need to increase all prices by 10%, you can create a formula in a new column to calculate the updated prices, then replace the original prices with the new values.

Keyboard Shortcuts for Editing:

- Familiarise yourself with keyboard shortcuts for editing tasks. For example, F2 to edit the active cell, Ctrl + D to fill down the contents of the topmost cell in a selected range, and Ctrl + R to fill right.

Leverage Sorting and Filtering:

- Use sorting (Data > Sort) and filtering (Data > Filter) to organise your data, making it easier to identify and edit sections of your dataset. Sorting

Skipton Tech

can help you group similar items together, while filtering allows you to display only the rows that meet certain criteria.

General Efficiency Practices

Keep a Clean Workspace:

- Regularly clean and organise your dataset. Remove any unnecessary rows, columns, or sheets to streamline your workbook and improve navigation and performance.

Use Templates for Recurring Projects:

- If you frequently work with similar datasets or reports, create templates with predefined formats, formulas, and settings. This saves time on setup and ensures consistency across similar projects.

Batch Process with Macros:

- For repetitive tasks, consider recording or writing macros to automate these processes. This can significantly speed up data editing, especially for complex or multi-step operations.

Adopting these tips for faster data entry and editing can dramatically improve your productivity in Excel.

By combining effective strategies with the software's built-in tools and features, you can streamline your workflow, reduce errors, and spend more time on analysis and decision-making.

Skipton Tech

Chapter 15

Troubleshooting Common Problems

Excel is a powerful tool for data analysis and reporting, but encountering errors, especially within formulas, is a common challenge for users. Understanding how to identify and resolve these errors is crucial for maintaining the integrity and accuracy of your data. This section focuses on dealing with common errors in formulas, providing strategies and insights to troubleshoot and correct them efficiently.

Dealing with Common Errors in Formulas

#DIV/0! Error - Division by Zero:

Cause: This error occurs when a formula attempts to divide a number by zero or an empty cell.
Solution: Check the divisor in your formula. If it's a reference to a cell, ensure that cell contains a non-zero value. Use the `IF` function to handle

potential zero values, e.g., `=IF(B2=0, "N/A", A2/B2)`.

#NAME? Error - Unrecognized Text in Formulas:

Cause: Excel displays this error when it doesn't recognize text in a formula. This can happen with misspelt function names, undefined named ranges, or missing quotation marks around text strings.
Solution: Double-check the spelling of functions and named ranges. Ensure that any text strings within your formula are enclosed in quotation marks.

#VALUE! Error - Incorrect Argument Type or Operand:

Cause: This error appears when a formula contains operands or arguments of a type that Excel wasn't expecting, such as using a text value in a calculation.
Solution: Verify the data types in your formula. Convert text to numbers if necessary using functions like `VALUE()` for text that represents numbers or `DATEVALUE()` for text that represents dates.

#REF! Error - Invalid Cell Reference:

Cause: The `#REF!` error signifies that a formula refers to a cell that's no longer valid. This often occurs after deleting cells or copying a formula that contains relative cell references.

Solution: Check the cell references in your formula. If you've deleted cells that were referenced, you may need to adjust your formula or restore the deleted data. Use absolute references (`$A$1`) if you plan to copy formulas.

#N/A Error - No Value Available:

Cause: This error is shown when a formula cannot find a referenced value. This is common with lookup functions like `VLOOKUP` or `HLOOKUP` when the lookup value isn't found.

Solution: Ensure the lookup value exists in the dataset. Consider using the `IFNA` function to provide a default value when the lookup fails, e.g., `=IFNA(VLOOKUP(...), "Not Found")`.

Circular Reference Warning:

Cause: A circular reference occurs when a formula refers to its own cell, either directly or through a chain of references. This can lead to an infinite loop, preventing Excel from calculating a result.

Solution: Excel usually highlights circular references. Locate the cell causing the issue and adjust the formula to eliminate the self-reference.

Review your calculations to ensure they logically flow without looping back to themselves.

Additional Tips for Troubleshooting Formulas

Using Formula Auditing Tools:

- Excel's Formula Auditing tools (on the Formulas tab) can help identify and correct errors. "Trace Precedents" and "Trace Dependents" show the relationships between cells and formulas, helping to pinpoint errors. "Evaluate Formula" lets you see how a formula is calculated step-by-step.

Watching Cell Values:

- The Watch Window (Formulas > Watch Window) allows you to monitor the values of specific cells as you edit other parts of your workbook. This is useful for troubleshooting formulas that depend on multiple inputs across your worksheet.

By familiarising yourself with common formula errors and learning how to use Excel's built-in tools for troubleshooting, you can enhance your proficiency in managing and analysing data. Effective error handling ensures your workbooks

are reliable, accurate, and trustworthy for
decision-making processes.